People
Speak
11

Chaim Walder

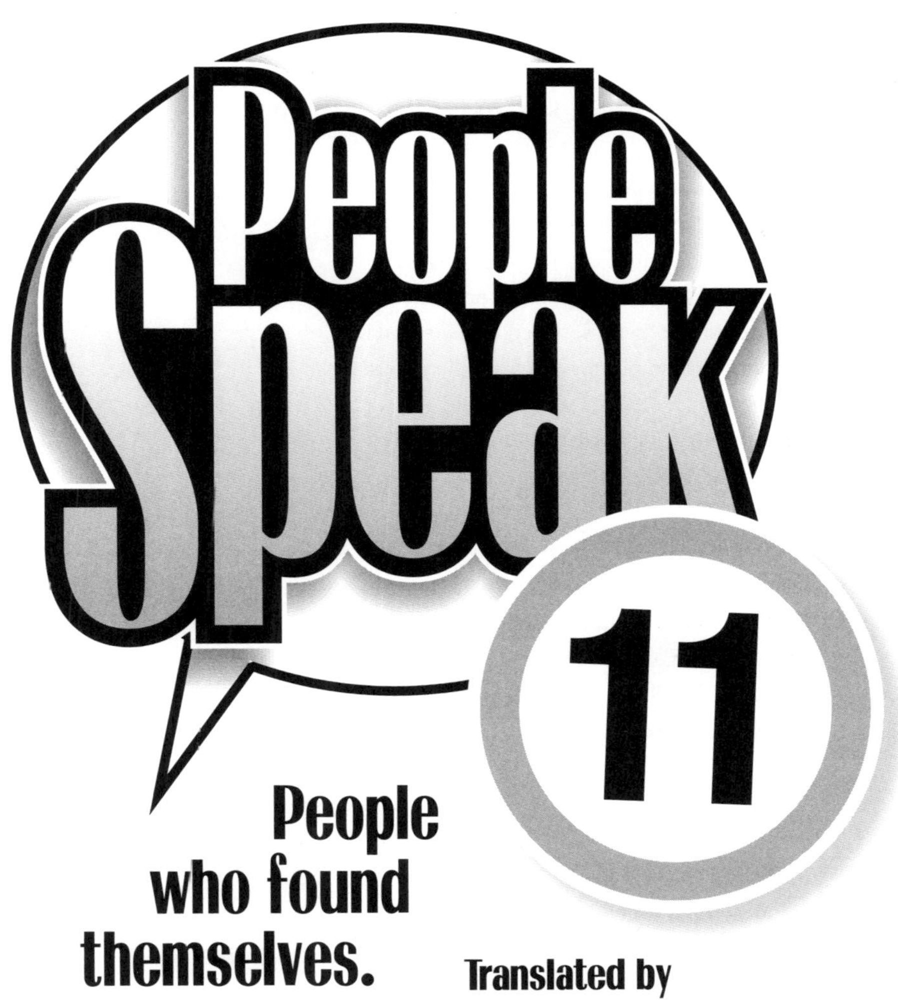

People who found themselves.

Translated by
Aviva Rappaport

FELDHEIM PUBLISHERS
JERUSALEM NEW YORK

ISBN 978-1-68025-435-8

Translated into English by Aviva Rappaport
Proofread by Cindy Scarr

DISTRIBUTED BY:
Feldheim Publishers
POB 43163 / Jerusalem, Israel
208 Airport Executive Park
Nanuet, NY 10954
www.feldheim.com

DISTRIBUTED IN EUROPE BY:
Lehmanns
+44-0-191-430-0333
info@lehmanns.co.uk
www.lehmanns.co.uk

DISTRIBUTED IN AUSTRALIA BY:
Golds World of Judaica
+613 95278775
info@golds.com.au
www.golds.com.au

Printed in Israel

Contents

Alone in the Desert

A group of yeshivah bachurim are lost on the Jordan Valley Road fifteen minutes before Shabbos. In that desolate place, they come upon a mysterious, seemingly abandoned place.

But that's just it. It only appears to be abandoned. Reality is about to give them the surprise of their lives.

My story is going to sound hard to believe, the product of a wild imagination. While it does contain thoughts and events that veer slightly from the rational, everything I'm about to tell you is one hundred percent true and can be verified.

It all happened some five years ago.

At the age of twenty-four, I was one of the older *bachurim* in the Diaspora Yeshivah headed by Rabbi Goldstein, *shlita*.

My room was one I'd wish on every *yeshivah bachur*: an apartment with a breathtaking view of David's Citadel and the

Old City. My roommates and I thought it was the most magical view ever—until the events of this story.

Chol hamoed Succos, I drove down to Tiveria together with a few friends. We davened at the tomb of Rabbi Meir Baal HaNess, slept in a cheap hostel, bought our own food, and had a great time.

I was a new driver then, so we rented a "*kollel* Subaru" for a few dollars. We split the cost of car rental, gas, and food, and if you've never seen penniless yeshivah students with no parental support dividing up expenditures, you don't know how petty things can get. Like, almost to the point of arguing over how many bites of challah you ate. Of course, the conversation is always conducted in a friendly spirit with sincere empathy for each other, because every single one of us was living from shekel to shekel, literally.

In other words, we were all broke. We tried hard not to take advantage of our parents, which wasn't difficult because the only thing our parents had plenty of was debts. Being in the same boat, we weren't too keen on acquiring more.

Friday arrived, which meant it was time to head back to our yeshivah for Shabbos *chol hamoed Succos*.

Here's where we made our first mistake. We left late, with only three hours to go before Shabbos, Yerushalayim time. The drive takes about two and a half hours, so that was cutting it close.

Once we were in the car, the question came up about which route to take. The shortest and simplest way to get from Tiveria to Yerushalayim is via Highway 6. But guess what? Highway 6 is a toll road. Using it would set us back around fifty shekels, and for guys who are totally broke, fifty shekels is

"I meant that I don't have a shekel for Highway 6," he shot back.

"And for a sheep that we have absolutely no use for, you *do* have twenty shekels?"

"Are you guys crazy? Do you know how much a sheep is worth? About ten thousand shekels!"

"Wow. Uh, what are you going to do with it?"

"I have no idea," he said. "But if you're offered ten thousand shekels worth of merchandise for twenty, you buy."

"Whatever you say," we said.

"What now?" someone asked.

Good question. By now, the Yerushalayim option was no longer relevant. Now we had to think about where we would make Shabbos. Staying where we were was not only impossible, but getting somewhere else was a matter of life or death considering the blazing sun, and that's even before we took into account the Palestinian Authority.

Suddenly, a police car drove up.

An officer got out and said, "There's a man accusing you of stealing his sheep."

"What?!" we exclaimed. "We didn't steal it. We bought it."

"Oh, you bought it? For how much?"

"Twenty shekels," the buyer replied, and without even thinking, all of us—including the officer—burst out laughing.

"It's true!" Nechemiah shouted and began to describe the bargaining process. Luckily no one heard him because we were all too busy laughing.

"Forget it," I told the officer. "Take the sheep. We don't have any use for it anyway." In the background, I heard Nechemiah protesting, but I ignored it. "The main thing is, we've got a problem. Our car died of thirst, and we're stuck here in the middle of nowhere without a place to spend Shabbos."

"He's not taking my sheep," Nechemiah interjected. "I bought it."

"I heard you," said the officer, who had pretty much written off Nechemiah. "You all stole a sheep, and now you expect me to help you?"

"We didn't steal any sheep," I said. "But I'm asking you to do this for us. And you know what? I think it was *hashgachah* that we met that Arab because without him bringing charges against us, you wouldn't be here, and then we'd really be stuck for Shabbos."

"The way I see it, you're still stuck for Shabbos," the officer replied.

"Wrong. You think we stole a sheep, so now you need to arrest us and put us in jail. At least we'll have a roof over our heads on Shabbos. You can't leave us here."

"Let me think," the officer said, and then fell silent for a moment. "You know what? Instead of arresting you, I'll take the sheep and return it."

Later we found out that this was a trick used often by the shepherds. They'd "sell" a sheep for next to nothing, usually around five hundred shekels, and then go to the police. Since it's against the law to transport sheep by car, the police confiscate the sheep and leave it on the side of the road. The shepherd ends up with both his sheep and the five hundred shekels. Or, in our out-of-the-box case, twenty.

"What about us?" I pressed.

"Well," the officer said, "fact is, there are no cities or settlements around here."

"So what should we do?" we asked him.

"Let me think," the officer said again. "Listen, there is some sort of a place nearby," he said finally, drawing the words out reluctantly. "I take no responsibility whatsoever. It's about ten minutes from here, and it's not a place I recommend to anyone, but I don't think you have much of a choice. It's some kind of a settlement where two people live. A couple. They're very—how should I put it?—eccentric. But you asked about a place where you could spend Shabbos, and maybe you'll be able to spend it there."

It sounded scary. An isolated place. Two eccentrics. In my imagination, I saw our bodies thrown into the field to land alongside hundreds of bodies dumped there over the years. (I know. My imagination was running wild. But that's what I felt.)

"I'm not sure..." I began hesitantly.

But Nechemiah jumped right in. "What do we have to lose? Let's go take a look."

"I'll drive you almost to the spot," the officer said. "You'll have to walk from there."

"What about our car?" I asked. "We can't just leave it here."

"You're right about that," the officer said. "Not a good idea. Let me think."

We waited impatiently.

"Look," he said finally. "I know someone around these parts with a four-wheel drive. I'll see if I can get him to tow your car over there. Meanwhile, get in."

We squeezed into his car, and Nechemiah said, "Wait! My sheep."

"You mean the sheep you stole."

"I told you, I didn't steal it. I bought it for twenty shekels."

The officer no longer argued. "Well, put it in my open trunk. I hope it doesn't fall out."

We stood the sheep in the open trunk and began our slow journey.

About ten minutes later, the officer stopped the car in the middle of nowhere. "Walk straight ahead," he said. "You'll see what looks like an oasis. That's where the place is."

"There's no sign?" we asked.

"There was. Made out of cardboard. But it gets stolen every so often."

It sounded just like what it sounds like. But on the other hand, what choice did we have?

We got out of the car, took the sheep, thanked the officer (who looked even more worried than we did) and started walking to...

We really had no idea where.

After walking through desert scrub, we saw a strange sight. It looked like a piece of village plunked down in the desert, with a house made of who knows what. It was as if we'd landed in some imaginary land with only three or four houses in it.

As we drew closer, we saw a house that had collapsed. I've probably lost you by now, but bear with me a little bit longer, and you'll see it's all true.

Now we saw a sign that gave the name of the place: "Beit Hogla across from Jericho."

We knocked here, we knocked there. No one answered.

There was another house. We knocked on its door too.

No one answered.

Nechemiah opened the door as if he owned the place. He said he seemed to hear a sound (just like he seemed to think he made the deal of a lifetime when he bought the sheep—which was still with us, by the way).

We went inside.

We entered a rather large room in which five beds were meticulously prepared. The place was clean and neat, sparkling and fresh smelling, with everything ironed to hotel-style perfection.

It was too crazy to be true.

"Maybe we died, and we're dreaming or something," said Mati.

We were still trying to figure out what to do when suddenly we heard a raspy voice behind us say, "Finally. You're here."

We cried out in fright and spun around to see who it was.

An old woman stood there.

"Welcome," she said. "We've been waiting for you."

"You've been waiting for *us*?"

"Yes, for you."

"Do you know us?"

"Not at all, but we knew you were coming."

Admit it. We should have run for our lives right then and there.

"We got stuck here," I said in a shaky voice.

"Yes," she said, "we're used to it. We were expecting you."

My mind raced as I imagined the fate of all the people they'd "expected" there. Any way I looked at it, it ended badly.

"Well," she said, "get yourselves settled in here. As you can see, we've made the beds for you. Actually, we were expecting five. That's what we need. But it's not so bad. We'll manage this way too."

We looked at each other in horror.

"What do you mean by 'we'll manage'?"

"There'll be a minyan," she said.

"A minyan?"

"Yes, a minyan," she said. "Along with my husband and you

four, we have another four not far from here, and we'll get the tenth somehow."

The word minyan restored our sanity somewhat.

"*Geveret*, can you please tell us what's going on here?"

"Gladly, but there's no time. I have to heat the food. I almost gave up. I thought that for the first time, we wouldn't have a minyan for Hoshana Rabbah, but Hashem always gives us one. I suggest you take showers and get ready for Shabbos. Meanwhile, I'm going to get everything ready. We only have twenty minutes."

"One second," I said. "About the food—"

"The chickens are Badatz, the vegetables are Gush Katif. I keep the bags, don't worry. My husband is more chareidi than you are."

There was a tiny shed with a shower. Somehow we got organized. Luckily, we had our *chol hamoed* clothes with us, which would work for Shabbos. So, just minutes before Shabbos, we were clean, polished, wearing a hat and a suit—and wondering how exactly a minyan would get there.

We walked outside to the succah, where we saw a man with a long beard who looked to be in his eighties, sitting and learning Gemara.

After we'd stood there staring for a few minutes, he closed his Gemara and said, "Follow me."

We walked in the desert for a few minutes and suddenly reached a small military base. There were about twenty soldiers, apparently guarding the area (this is an area that borders the Palestinian Authority). We managed to get five soldiers to join us for the minyan.

After Maariv, we returned to Beit Hogla, where a feast fit for a king awaited us. Who would have believed it? In our wildest dreams, we couldn't have imagined such a thing happening. We sang for three hours, and between the songs they told us the story of this mysterious place called "Beit Hogla."

The outpost was built by Yosef and Erna Kobos, who operated the ancient Shalom Al Yisrael Synagogue in Jericho, making sure there were always services with a minyan as well as classes.

And then came the Oslo Accords.

They were supposed to make peace with Israel, but when the territory was transferred to the Palestinian Authority, the first thing the PA did, as expected, was burn down the shul that had been cared for by the couple. The Shalom Al Yisrael went up in flames, and not only metaphorically.

The couple and their friends established an enclave called Nachal Elisha, and from there they traveled to Jericho to renovate and restore the synagogue, resuming services and classes. Seven months later, they were evacuated by the army. They returned and were again evacuated until the army deigned to give them an area near "Nebo Camp," the military camp we were in. They called the place Beit Hogla after the ancient city located on the border of the area allocated to the tribe of Benjamin: "And the border passed along to the side of Beit Hogla northward..." (*Yehoshua* 18:19).

Initially, several families called the place home, but they left because of the harsh conditions in the dangerous, desolate desert. Only the Koboses remained, producing olive oil and pomegranate juice like you've never tasted in your life, and of course, taking care of the Shalom Al Yisrael Synagogue.

Our host told us that only a week earlier, Arabs had infiltrated the place, tied them up, and taken all their horses and donkeys.

"We stayed tied up for twenty-four hours," he said, "until, with *siyatta diShemaya*, a soldier who wanted pomegranate juice arrived and discovered us tied up and starving."

He told the story in an amused tone, not noticing the terror on the faces of the four guys whose imagination ran wild as they visualized what could have happened to them if they stayed there stuck on the road all night. Even Mati was white.

"We have an agreement with the army and the Palestinian Authority that once a year we are allowed to enter the synagogue, accompanied, of course, by the army, to conduct a religious activity. We chose Hoshana Rabbah as the day.

"The first few years, about two hundred people came. We'd learn through the night, daven, dance, and have *seudos*. Over the years, fewer and fewer people came. Even our children fled. But there was always a minyan. One way or the other, we always had people drop in, so we always prepared for a minyan.

"This Shabbos, too, my wife prepared the guest room in the hopes that people would come. But Shabbos rapidly approached with no one in sight. I dressed for Shabbos, but before going out to the succah, I told my wife, 'That's it. It's all over. There won't be any minyan. We're really alone.'

"Then you showed up to give us another joyous *chol hamoed Succos* plus Hoshana Rabbah in the Shalom Al Israel Synagogue."

No one spoke.

"In case you were wondering, the learning will take place here in my succah, and tomorrow we'll go to the synagogue to daven. You realize, of course, that you didn't just 'happen' to end up here."

Motza'ei Shabbos arrived. Our rosh yeshivah, Rabbi Avraham Goldstein, called us in a panic.

"Where have you been? We were worried about you."

We told him the whole story. He got very excited. "I'm coming to Jericho with some students, and we'll all celebrate Hoshana Rabbah at the Shalom Al Yisrael Synagogue."

And that's what happened. On Hoshana Rabbah night, we learned in the succah with a special intensity I'd never felt before. I strongly felt that Hashem had guided us to this very place.

In the morning, when we got into the car and started it, the engine sprang to life without a problem. (Okay, there was a reason it had gotten stuck.) We drove to Jericho, which was only fifteen minutes away. We entered the synagogue in awe and davened with Rabbi Goldstein and others. There were *hakafos*, "*Kol mevaser, mevaser v'omer*," beating the *aravos*, and a *seudah*.

It was the most meaningful Hoshana Rabbah I've ever experienced.

If the story seems unreal, you're invited to visit Beit Hogla yourself. It's located…uh…actually, I'm not sure where. But it's for sure somewhere on the Jordan Valley Road south of Beit Shean. There's probably a cardboard sign or maybe now a wooden one. Then again, it's equally probable that someone may have just stolen it.

I'm married now, with a son, and I organize *kiruv* events all over the country. Whenever I travel the Jordan Valley Road, I always stop by Beit Hogla for a drink of the amazing pomegranate juice made by Mrs. Orna Kobos.

And what happened to the sheep? It wandered around the Diaspora Yeshiva for a while. Nechemiah was very attached to it even though everyone blamed it for the whole thing.

Then one day, a bearded man dressed in rags arrived and wanted to know if he could buy the sheep for his son's bris.

Nechemiah said he was ready and willing to sell it to him. The man said he didn't have more than five hundred shekels.

"Twenty shekels and it's yours," Nechemiah told him.

The man's jaw dropped. He pulled a twenty-shekel bill from his pocket and handed it over, then disappeared with the sheep before Nechemiah could change his mind.

Thanks to Yitzik Batzun ("*Hafakah Memuteget*") for this amazing story.

"He Looks at the Earth and It Quakes"

The manager of a post office branch faces a customer who humiliates him publicly and shames him in front of his coworkers and customers. He could have responded as would most people. Instead, he chooses to respond in the exact opposite way.

What happens next is a real earthquake.

I've been with the post office for the past twenty-five years and the manager of a post office branch for a decade. I don't think it's hard to describe what the job demands. It's a difficult, challenging position that comes with a lot of stress. There are never enough workers to get the job done, and there's never enough time to do it in.

At the post office, as opposed to other government branches, promptness is of the essence. People who mail letters and packages want them to arrive on time.

I guess plenty of people will laugh at my putting the words "post office" and "promptness" together, especially during the period I'm talking about when the situation was a catastrophe due to changes that took place in the organization. The people who bore the brunt of the anger at those changes were the workers in the field, from the managers right on down to the mailmen. The big executives stayed in their air-conditioned offices showing each other pie charts of the amazing results they were getting from the changes they'd made.

As a branch manager, you have dozens of decisions to make every second, from making sure enough clerks are manning the customer service windows to arranging postal bank transfers to sorting packages and putting mail in post office boxes. Actually, I was a manager, a clerk, and a sorter, all at once—in addition to doing any and every other job that needed to get done—because the pressure doesn't let you sit in an office for a minute.

The story I want to tell you happened two years ago. To be exact, it took place on Tuesday 28 Elul/September 19, 2017, two days before Rosh Hashanah 5778. There is significance to this date.

That afternoon, a customer walked in and asked to send money to Mexico.

Western Union offers a money transfer service. If you want to send money anywhere in the world (until recently, even to Iran), all you have to do is walk into any post office in Israel, deposit the money, and request a transfer. Within hours, the person to whom you sent the money can walk into any Western Union branch and receive the money. Plain and simple.

So, this customer walked in with five thousand dollars and asked to make a transfer to his father-in-law in Mexico.

The clerk tried to make the transfer, but there was a computer glitch, and the transfer didn't go through.

Meanwhile, the line wasn't moving. More people came in, and it was getting crowded. People started grumbling.

After a few more unsuccessful tries, I told the clerk to let it go and move on to the other customers in line.

"Wait! I'm first," the customer said to me.

"Yes," I explained to him, "but there's some kind of a problem, and we can't make everyone else wait."

The man raised his voice. "What you're doing is wrong!"

I tried to be courteous. "I'm sorry, sir, but other customers are waiting for the clerk, and your transfer cannot be completed right now. Please wait a few minutes. I promise you we'll try again."

The man waited, eight customers were served, and then I told the clerk to take care of his transfer again.

But once again, the transfer didn't go through. I tried to help, but we kept getting an error message. We didn't know what to do.

Meanwhile, the man was talking on his cell phone with his father-in-law, speaking rapid Hebrew in a loud voice. No way was this a private conversation. No, he made sure that every single person in the post office heard every single word.

"Are you listening? I'm here at the worst post office in the country with the worst manager in the country! I've never seen someone so unprofessional." That's what he announced to his father-in-law, and the entire post office with all its employees and customers heard it loud and clear. Some customers appeared to be enjoying my humiliation since they also bore a grudge against the post office, and what could be more satisfying than to watch someone else let out his frustrations on me?

The man relished the role he'd taken on himself and began to fancy himself a reporter reporting live at a major event. Loud enough for everyone to follow every single word, he broadcast a blow-by-blow account of every move I made, adding commentary about how slowly I was working and how poorly I ran the branch in general.

I can't say it didn't affect me. He was trashing me in public. He had a sharp tongue and a cruel one and knew how to do it to perfection.

We tried to help him a third time, but again, the same glitch happened. I called other branches, but they reported no malfunctions in their computer systems. Then again, they weren't trying to transfer money to Mexico. We had no way of knowing if the problem was with the system at our branch or with Mexico.

And the man didn't stop his abuse and insults.

I'd never met a person so verbally abusive. When I say abusive, you probably imagine someone screaming or cursing, but it wasn't that. His words were refined. He described me clinically, as a psychologist might describe a patient. On second thought, psychologists respect their patients. He was ridiculing me with well-honed cynicism. In fact, he described for his audience how I probably acted at home, what kind of person I was. He also told them—as he imagined it, of course—how I got my job. Someone used pull to get me a job at the post office after failing to push me in anywhere else.

I'm deliberately describing at length the hurt and humiliation to share with you what I went through right then. But believe me, no matter what lengths I would go to describe it, I'll never come close to giving you the full picture of what went on there.

It's said that one who causes the blood to drain from another person's face by humiliating him is considered to have shed his blood, and that's exactly how I felt. I was put down publicly for all to see, and not a single person came to my defense.

I judge them favorably, though. At that time, Israel Post

functioned at a very low level due to all the radical changes imposed on it from the higher-ups. Now I knew how the crowd must have felt while witnessing the incident of Kamtza and Bar Kamtza, when they didn't intervene to prevent the disgracing of Bar Kamtza. They were quiet because they enjoyed seeing him humiliated.

Still, I had hoped someone would come to my defense.

I think I was hurt mostly because my workers—the people who work under me—witnessed it. One worker did try to silence the man, but he, too, came under attack. A few well-placed barbs stunned him into silence, leaving the attacker free to return his attention to me.

Closing time arrived. I had to inform the man that the transfer would not take place that day, but that if he wanted to, he could try coming the following morning, and hopefully we'd be able to do it then.

"Forget it. I'm not setting foot in this place again." Then he found something more sophisticated to say: "No, I take that back. I *will* set foot in here, but only on the day you *don't* set foot in here. And I hereby inform you that that day will not be long in coming. I won't give up until you're kicked out of here—and hopefully from Israel Post entirely—in disgrace. You're an embarrassment to the institution. I'll make sure your superiors know about this."

And then he left.

We were all still there, the employees. An awkward silence hung in the air. A few clerks looked distraught, and I felt crushed. I didn't know what to do with what had happened there. I also felt enraged to the point of burning anger toward that man who'd heaped abuse on me in public. He'd hurt my feelings deeply, and put me down in front of my workers and the whole crowd of people waiting for service. What do you do with feelings like those?

And then...

An idea popped into my mind.

Among the staff was a woman who'd been married for twelve years and hadn't been blessed with children. What hadn't we done for her! We'd taken upon ourselves *kabbalos* and divided up *sefer Tehillim*, but nothing happened.

I suddenly found myself crying out, "I forgive this man and dedicate everything I just went through to—" here I named the employee along with her mother's name "—and her husband to be blessed with children!"

Tears filled the eyes of all the employees. Only someone who was there could understand what a gift I gave her. The kind of humiliation to which I was subjected is something people find hard to forgive even decades later, yet I took it, fresh and bloody, and presented it as an offering for the welfare of a childless couple.

Strangely, this made things easier for me, too.

We closed up and headed home.

That night, I couldn't fall asleep.

The public tongue-lashing that man had given me tormented me and made me burst into tears from time to time. And I'm not a man who cries.

I tried to hide what I was going through from my wife, both to spare her and also because it was too hard for me to share it with anyone.

Morning came, and I went out to daven and go to the post office.

The workers opened the customer service windows, half an hour passed, and suddenly, in burst the verbally abusive man of the day before.

You could have heard a pin drop.

Had he come back to continue his tirade?

No. He strode over to me, shook my hand, gave me a warm hug, and said, "I want to apologize to you for the way I acted toward you yesterday. I'm really sorry. I don't know what came over me. I'll do anything for you to forgive me."

I looked at him, amazed. I didn't understand what was going on with him.

The truth is that at first, I thought he was dishing out yesterday's abuse, just serving it up with more style.

But no, the man was completely serious.

"You're not going to believe this," he said excitedly. "As you know, my father-in-law was waiting at home for a call from me telling him I'd made the transfer. He would need to go to an office building where Western Union was located to get the money, but as long as I didn't give him the go-ahead that the transfer was made, he saw no point in going there.

"Just minutes after I left here, about the time my father-in-law would have been at the Western Union office if the money order had gone through, an earthquake of a magnitude 7.1 on the Richter scale took place in Mexico City. Dozens of buildings collapsed, including the office building where my father-in-law was supposed to pick up the money. Hundreds of people were killed!

"I was upset with you, but all along it was G-d Himself Who prevented the deposit from going through to save my father-in-law's life. I'm ashamed of the way I treated you.

"I know you can't forgive me for what I did, and there's no way to repair the damage because there was a big crowd present. But I'm willing to stand here and apologize to everyone if only you'll say you forgive me."

I remained silent.

"It's okay," one of my workers said. "He already forgave you."

"What do you mean?"

"Yesterday, after you left, he announced that he forgave you for all the humiliation and was giving the merit for doing so to one of our coworkers who's still childless after twelve years of marriage."

The man looked at me.

He was speechless.

Suddenly he burst into wracking sobs.

"How wicked I am," he said to me, "and how righteous you are. I hurt you when you hadn't done anything wrong, while you… Not only didn't you respond in kind, you even forgave me!

"I hope I can repent for the way I treated you, and I promise to pray for that employee."

He turned to leave but stopped at the entrance and said, "I'll never forget what I learned from you here."

And then he was gone.

And now comes the best part.

Exactly nine and a half months after this took place, the employee had a baby girl! Yes, the one who was childless for a dozen years. And every single employee at our post office knew why and in what merit this miracle took place.

The Creator spins His world on its axis as He wishes. He caused a glitch in our computer so that a meritorious Jew in

Mexico didn't leave his house to pick up a money order so that he wouldn't find himself at the center of an earthquake that would snuff out his life.

He sent a fellow here to humiliate me as no one in my entire life has ever humiliated me so that I could gift my forgiveness to a childless couple.

And now, if anyone has any doubts about the amazing *hashgachah pratis* that surrounds us constantly, let him come to me. I'll tell him the story I just shared with you.

Lost in Lebanon

What's an ordinary citizen doing driving through a battle zone during the Lebanon War in a tank missing its caterpillar track?

What is it that troubles a Lebanese family from the town of Bhamdoun?

And why a mikvah on a mountain overlooking Beirut?

An unbelievable story about unbelievable people.

My story is one of the most unusual stories you've ever heard in your life. Not only that, but the amazing ending comes as a total surprise. It took place over thirty-five years ago.

Nowadays, I'm retired. I fought in Israel's three best-known wars: the Six Day War, where I was privileged to be among those who liberated Jerusalem and the Western Wall; the Yom Kippur War; and the Lebanon War.

The story I want to tell you happened in the last war I

fought in, actually the last "real" war to take place here: the 1982 Lebanon War, also known as Operation Peace for Galilee, during which 657 Israeli soldiers were killed and thousands wounded. The wars that followed (without in any way disparaging the wars or the soldiers who fought in them), the Second Lebanon War (2006), and operations Defensive Shield and Cast Lead, were not really "wars."

I was injured in the early days of the war and could have been discharged, but I wanted nothing more than to escape from the hospital to return to my unit.

We crossed the border with Lebanon near Rosh Hanikra, and then we drove along the Lebanese coastal road. Picture driving up the Israeli coastal road, from Nahariya to Achziv Beach to Rosh Hanikra and continuing northward.

We were traveling along the Lebanese coastal road when heavy shelling suddenly hit us as the entire Lebanese coast was bombarded. We stopped to take shelter and waited for our forces to somehow put an end to the shelling.

Then, from inside our tank, we spotted an Israeli tank on the verge of collapse. We knew that whoever was inside it was in big trouble, but we couldn't move from where we'd taken shelter.

You're probably wondering why, if it's a tank, it would be in trouble.

That's just it. This wasn't the kind of tank you're picturing. In fact, I may now be subject to a lawsuit by tank manufacturers for calling that huge pickup truck a tank. Let me just say in my defense that there wasn't a single member of our battalion who didn't know it was a tank even though they knew it wasn't a tank.

Confused?

Okay, so it was a Chabad mitzvah tank.

I guess the driver thought that if Chabad goes everywhere, that meant it had to get to Lebanon, too.

Someone motioned for him to take shelter near us. That didn't happen. Instead, a Chabad chassid popped out of the tank and asked, "Where are you headed?" as if he was on a nice, quiet beach somewhere with blue waves lapping at the sand. Actually, he *was* on a nice, quiet beach. Except that the shells landing on it were less quiet, and the color they made was more like red.

We waved our arms to signal him to flee. He rushed back into his "tank" and drove it closer to where we had taken shelter.

"What are you doing here?!" someone yelled out to him.

"I came to help you put on tefillin," he said nonchalantly as if the questioner was truly interested in what he was doing.

The officer who asked couldn't clarify that he wasn't really asking but accusing. That's because the entire battalion had already surrounded the Chabad "tank," asking the chassid to help them put on tefillin. He'd already appointed himself helpers and assistant helpers who knew how to help others put on tefillin, so the chain of command was quickly blurred.

Even those to whom the idea of putting on tefillin didn't speak stood in line because everyone who put on tefillin got some vodka as well. Either way, the tefillin and the vodka did their thing, and about half an hour later, bombardment or not, the entire battalion broke out into a joyful dance.

Eventually, the shelling stopped, and we were ordered to proceed north toward Beirut, the capital of Lebanon.

The road to Beirut wasn't strewn with roses, and at a certain point, it became impossible to continue. Accordingly, we received an order to head up into the mountains, with the intention of controlling the roads leading to Beirut and then conquering the city.

We started climbing, some of us by foot and some with heavy equipment, up mountains over 3,000 feet high. My company and I approached a town called Bhamdoun, where our story takes place.

When we arrived in Bhamdoun, we set ourselves up in the local stadium and awaited our orders.

As we were getting organized, a woman walked into the stadium, and after engaging her in conversation to find out who she was and what she was, they called me over to speak with her.

I had no idea why I was called, but as soon as she began talking, I understood. She made a request that was the most unimaginable request I could imagine in an enemy country, and in a backwater city named Bhamdoun.

She spoke Hebrew, said she was Jewish, and wanted someone religious to help the community build a mikvah.

It took me a while to answer. And no, I didn't reply to her request for the mikvah. "What in the world are you doing here?" is what I said. "This country is a dangerous place for Jews, and it's about to become a lot more dangerous. Come to Israel, where your community will have as many mikvahs as it wants."

She told me they had been offered this many times before, and some members of their family had already immigrated to Israel, some to the United States, but she and others had remained in Lebanon.

She said that until recently they had lived in Beirut, where they also had a synagogue. There, they used the sea for immersion, but recently, terrorists had taken over Beirut (back then, the terrorists were Fatah, led by Yasser Arafat; Hezbollah didn't exist yet). It was strongly recommended that they disappear from Beirut before being taken to the sea, and not for immersion. So they fled to Bhamdoun, and here they found it difficult to build a mikvah.

I begged her to leave the area. "It's a dangerous place," I explained to her.

She listened to me patiently, and I was sure she was convinced, but when I was finished she asked, "So can you arrange a mikvah for us?"

I shrugged and said, "Lady, I can't do anything now, but I promise you I'll do what I can, and that's not much."

That was the truth right then.

We scattered there on the mountains to take up positions, and after two weeks, Nachal soldiers replaced us. On the way back from Bhamdoun, on one of the narrow roads, we again saw a tank. A Chabad tank, of course. Same driver, wandering around Lebanon as if it were Kfar Chabad.

I went over to the chassid and said to him, "Look, there's some Jewish woman up there who claims they need a mikvah. Can you take care of it?"

What do you think he said? "Sure thing. A tank driver talked to me about it. He said there are Jews in Bhamdoun who want a mikvah. We're thinking about what to do."

"A tank driver," I repeat.

"Uh, not a tank like mine. I mean a plain old army tank."

Believe me, the guy said it with a straight face. He believed with all his heart and soul that his battered "tank" was worth more than a Merkava Mark III, a battle tank worth $3.5 million. In fact, as the war went on and took a terrible casualty toll, *everyone* began to understand it.

The war ended. Actually, it didn't end until 2000, and over the next 16 years, the IDF sank into the Lebanese mud and absorbed 559 more casualties, until it withdrew under Ehud Barak's command.

I returned home, but I never forgot that town in Lebanon, Bhamdoun, and certainly not that poor woman, whom I was certain was no longer among the living. You see, like everyone else, I read the reports that Lebanon was razed to the ground, and towns like Bhamdoun and its surroundings became islands of destruction. The situation of the Jews, which was also bad, became even worse after the Sabra and Shatila massacre that same year, in which Christian soldiers massacred about 1,000 civilians in two Muslim refugee camps. The world, of course, with the help of Israeli leftists, blamed Israel for the massacre, even though IDF soldiers played no part in it. Hatred for Jews increased worldwide, not to mention in Lebanon itself. Bhamdoun is a short drive from the refugee camps, and I knew there was no way the woman and her family could have survived.

For years I had a hard time falling asleep because my mind kept replaying the harsh sights I saw in Lebanon. And there were always moments when my heart twisted in agony, though I knew I bore no guilt and had warned her to flee. Still, my conscience gave me no peace. It bothered me that I hadn't warned her in more explicit terms. Why hadn't I done something to save her and her family?

Many years have passed since then. I've married off all my children, some of whom are serious full-time learners in *kollel*, yet this matter remained an open wound.

A few years ago, I was driving with my son, who learns in

kollel in Bnei Brak, and a few other *avreichim*. I have a big van, and I enjoy helping people by giving them rides.

These were *avreichim* I'd been giving rides to for years, and I knew them all by name.

Over the years, we'd talk about this and that. All sorts of topics came up.

One day, as we were driving home from the *kollel*, I spotted a notice plastered on a wall. I stopped the van to read it and couldn't tear my eyes away.

One of my passengers became curious and asked me what the notice was about. I replied that it was a notice about a fund-raising campaign to build mikvahs.

The fellow was silent for a few seconds and then said, "Now I'm even more curious. I mean, there are fundraising campaigns like that every day. What's so interesting about this one?"

"Because it's about building mikvahs," I said.

A thick silence filled the car, which made me realize that my answers were only adding to the confusion and not the opposite.

"Do you really want to know why it interests me?"

"Of course we do," several said.

"Then I'll tell you," I said. "But don't come to me later complaining that I wasted your time."

And then I told them my story, about the Lebanon War, about my injury, about coming to Bhamdoun, about the Jewish woman who asked me for a mikvah, and about my double pain over the years because not only did I not give her a mikvah but I didn't tell her strongly enough how dangerous the situation was and so most likely she and her family met their deaths there, either at the hands of the Muslims or the Christians in all the terrible chaos during those years in Lebanon.

Suddenly, as I was talking and driving, one of the important *avreichim* traveling with me, a serious person who didn't talk much, said, "I might be able to give you details about this woman."

"How would you know any details?" I asked in surprise.

"I'm Lebanese," he said. "My brothers and sisters were born there. I have no idea where they lived, but if you want to stop by my parents' house, we could hear the details from them."

"Where do your parents live?"

"Three blocks from here."

"Do the rest of you want me to let you off first before I go there?" I asked everyone else.

"We're curious about the story. Let's stop at his parents' house first."

Another two minutes of driving and we were at the house. I parked.

"Give me a couple of minutes," he said. "I'll go up and ask my mother for the details."

We waited a full five minutes. I felt a little uncomfortable at having the *avreichim* wait like that, but they really wanted to know if their friend's parents knew anything about what had happened to that woman.

When he came out of the building, he wasn't alone.

His mother was with him.

I took one look at her and cried, "It's impossible!" I jumped out of the car and ran to them.

His mother was the same woman I met in Bhamdoun. The decades had failed to blur my memory.

In case this sounds too far-fetched, I'll tell you the family name: the Luzia family of Bnei Brak. Eli and Mazal Luzia.

I stood there on the sidewalk, crying. The sobs burst out of me like never before. I'd never cried like that. *Never.* A heavy burden had been weighing me down for so many years. I was sure the woman was no longer alive, and every time the incident came to mind, I was tormented by feelings of guilt. And now, out of the blue, standing there in front of me alive and well was that very same woman. And not only that, but she was the mother of a *kollel* guy I'd been giving rides to for years. It was too much.

After I'd calmed down, she told us the whole story.

Apparently, the religious tank driver's efforts bore fruit. The Chabadniks arrived in their mitzvah tank at Bhamdoun, and within a few weeks took care of the mikvah. There *was* a mikvah in the town, but it couldn't be used because it was filled with rubble and debris. They located it, repaired it, and made it kosher. They even brought in blocks of ice, apparently made from water suitable for a mikvah, to add to the regular water, and the mikvah was up and running.

They didn't stop there, either. They paid for heating the mikvah, too. That's how devoted the Chabadniks were to the few Jews who lived in Bhamdoun.

We learned from the woman's story that the connection I made between this community and the mitzvah tank driver ultimately saved their lives.

Through him, they developed a very special relationship with the Rabbi of Tzfas at the time, Rabbi Levi Bistrisky, *ztz"l.*

Rabbi Bistrisky arranged for the family to be given plane tickets to New York to spend Succos with the Rebbe, which wasn't easy because by then the United States was reluctant to admit Lebanese citizens. During the visit, the Rebbe asked that Eli, who is a kohen, bless him, and then he gave them a silver Kiddush cup and spoke with them in French.

When he heard that they wanted to return to Lebanon, he told them, "It's forbidden for you to return to Lebanon."

Eli told the rabbi, "But we have a lot of businesses in Lebanon. How about if we go back for a few months to sell our holdings?"

The Rebbe was adamant. "You will not set foot in Lebanon," he said and blessed them with a successful aliyah to Eretz Yisrael.

Eli and Mazal left him feeling confused, but the people with them told them, "It's best that you listen to what he said. You won't regret it."

They stayed awake the whole night, and in the end, made the hardest decision they'd ever made in their lives: to immigrate to Israel without first going back to Lebanon to sell their property or businesses.

They came to Eretz Yisrael poor and destitute. The first few months were unbearable, but then something happened that made them understand the whole move.

As I told you, from September 16 to September 18, 1982, Christian Phalangists entered the Sabra and Shatila refugee camps near Beirut and massacred the residents. The massacre inflamed Muslim hatred against the Christians, and even more so against the Jews, whom the world blamed for the massacre. The Israeli leftists even formed an investigative committee that accused Defense Minister Ariel Sharon of the massacre and drove him out of office.

"Every resident of Bhamdoun was slaughtered. Not one single person was left," the woman said. "If we had stayed there, our family would have been wiped off the face of the earth. And here we are, thanks to the fact that you made contact with the Chabad people, and of course thanks to Rabbi Bistrisky and the

Lubavitcher Rebbe, *zy"a*. If not for him, we would have returned to Lebanon."

That's the story.

A soldier arrived in the middle of nowhere in Lebanon and merited to be a small link in the chain of connection between an anonymous Jewish woman and the driver of a "tank" not worth even the tread of a real tank but worth a whole platoon of tanks.

It is also a story of a circle that closed miraculously when the *avreich* he gave a ride to nearly every day for years turned out to be the son of that family, whose fate tormented this soldier night after night for many years.

My name is Jacob Citron of Bnei Brak, and that soldier is me.

"Open Your Hand and Sustain"

A family is dealing with a neighbor who takes advantage of them. She doesn't just "borrow" bread and milk, she consumes them regularly. Their home has become her mini-mart.

You might have put her in her place—which is why you should read this story.

I grew up in a suburb in the center of the country. It's an unpretentious place whose residents are simple working people.

My parents were good people who worked hard to support us. They barely managed to scrape by, but they maintained our home and family in a respectable manner. What filled the gaps was a lot of love and giving. And a good education, mostly by personal example.

We kids had some struggles along the way, especially when we didn't get all the things our friends did. But even if it was somewhat annoying now and then, we tried hard to deal with it on our own and certainly didn't pressure our parents for things they couldn't afford to buy us.

And now, about our neighbor.

She was raising three children alone, and, like my mother, she also worked as a cleaning lady. But that's where the similarity ends.

This neighbor didn't really know how to bring up her children. They spent lots of time playing outside, and though her financial situation was worse than ours, she'd buy them the best clothes and toys, which put her in debt.

We knew this because in a neighborhood like ours, there were no secrets. Also, because she'd come crying to my mother about her difficult situation. My mother would listen to her and offer encouragement. I remember her crying to my mother about an unpaid bill at the grocery store and telling her how she was ashamed to shop there. I also remember the time when, after she left, my sister said to our mother, "Why didn't you tell her it was wrong to buy such an expensive bike for her son if she had no money to buy food?"

Ima explained to us that there are people who don't know how to manage money. If she lectured this neighbor, Ima told us, it wouldn't do a thing to change the neighbor's habits. It would only make her upset and cause a rift between them.

Two weeks later, the neighbor complained to my mother about one of the other neighbors who had made a remark about her spending too much on shoes for one of her children. "You have no money for falafel, so what's your game?" he'd said. She was hurt to the depths of her soul and no longer spoke to those neighbors.

And we saw how right Ima was.

At a certain point, the neighbor began "borrowing" food.

In most places, it's common for people to knock on a neighbor's door and ask to borrow eggs, milk, sugar, or salt. We heard that in wealthy areas, it's not all that usual. My mother used to say with a laugh, "I guess that's why they're rich." But by us, people gave generously.

Our neighbor, though, took it to another level entirely. Because she owed money at the grocery store, she started coming to us to borrow milk, vegetables, cheese, and bread.

What started out as a little here and a little there turned into a permanent arrangement. She might stop by four times a day and ask, "Can I borrow three tomatoes? A dozen eggs? Nine-percent cream cheese?"

At first, we thought it was funny, but we soon realized this was no joke. It started to bother us.

"Ima, she borrows without returning," we said.

But my mother told us, "When someone asks for food, you never refuse them."

Slowly but surely, it became a routine. Four or five times a day, the neighbor would knock on our door to ask for things. At times it was irritating, like when her son showed off his new mountain bike or all kinds of expensive toys she'd bought him, when we knew we lived hand to mouth and that Abba sweated and slaved doing renovations, and our mother cleaning, just to let us live in dignity.

How many times had we tried to tell Ima that things couldn't go on like this and that it irritated us no end. But she wouldn't budge. "When someone asks for food, you give it to them."

One day, Ima said to the neighbor, "Why should you have

to knock on our door? Make yourself at home. Come on in and open the refrigerator and take what you need."

We thought Ima was being sarcastic, but then we realized she wasn't. *She's probably just trying to make her feel good*, we thought. But the neighbor took our mother's words at face value, and from then on, we'd hear a small tap, the front door would open, and the neighbor would walk right in and take whatever she wanted.

In case you can't imagine how annoying this could be, I'll try to give you an idea. Let's say you arrive home planning to have a cup of coffee, but when you open the refrigerator, you discover there's no milk. So you go to the neighbor and, in the best-case scenario, she pours you a glass of milk from the bag she took from *your* refrigerator. And in the worst-case scenario, she says, "I've got just one cup left, and Yoram needs it for dinner."

One day, the neighbor came into our house at ten in the morning.

She said hello, but no one answered.

She didn't understand why the house was empty and the door unlocked. "Is anybody home?" she called out.

She heard muffled sounds from the back rooms and decided to go see what was happening there.

In the hallway next to the bedrooms, she saw my father lying on the floor, moaning.

She quickly called an ambulance. The ambulance rushed my father to the hospital, where they saved his life.

He'd had a heart attack. Another five minutes, and we would have found him lifeless.

In one minute, the whole picture snapped into focus.

We were resentful because we thought we were being taken advantage of. We were furious and felt that we were being exploited. But He Who sits on High had the last laugh and sent us proof that you never lose out from doing a kindness and that the approach of my dear mother, not withholding food from anyone who asks, even if he doesn't deserve it and even if he doesn't return it, is what kept our father alive.

I was eleven when this happened. My parents were the most important thing in my life. I can't think of what would have happened to me if I had lost my father at that age. He was given back to me as a gift.

From then on, my father no longer did renovations since he was now disabled. The financial situation at home grew even worse, but that didn't stop my mother from continuing her open-door policy—and this time, we didn't say a word. And not only did we not say anything, we no longer thought it was wrong.

The neighbor kept coming and taking, and we somehow got along financially between my mother's work and my father's disability allowance.

But the story doesn't end here.

Two years later, the neighbor rescued my father again. And in exactly the same way. She came to take something and found him unconscious after a massive heart attack. She was there just to save him. His and my mother's good deeds are what brought the Angel Raphael to save my father.

From then on, we didn't take any chances. An emergency call button was installed in the house, replaced a few years later with an innovative device that could detect a heart attack before it occurred.

My father suffered from congestive heart failure, but at least he lived and contributed greatly to the home, in his own way. My mother continued to work, and as we got older and more mature, we started earning money too.

Fourteen years after the first heart attack, I married. That was two years ago. My father walked me to the chuppah, and our hearts were filled with joy.

At that time, the neighbor and her children moved to another city. She found easier work as a housekeeper and somehow scraped by. Now there was no one to walk into our house and enjoy our food. You'd be surprised how hard this was for my mother.

A year ago, my father had another heart attack, his final one. My mother was at his side, but it didn't help.

It came as no surprise. We'd known it wouldn't be long before he'd be asked to return his soul to the Creator. He had a distinguished funeral, and although I was and still am in deep sorrow and mourning for the dearest person I ever knew, I realized that I'd been granted a gift of fifteen years with my father at the most crucial time of my life, from the age of eleven to twenty-six. I was able to grow up with my father still there to guide me and let me learn from his beautiful *middos*.

Today I view this neighbor as sent by Hashem to keep my father alive, and this story opened my eyes to realize just how complex the world is. I hope that when you tell it, it will inspire everyone to look for the bigger picture, even the parts we can't see at the time, and help them realize that you never lose out by doing *chesed*.

On Shabbos when my husband sings *Eishes Chayil*, two verses in particular never fail to bring tears to my eyes: "She holds out her hand to the poor, and extends her hands to the destitute" and "Her husband's heart trusts in her and only profits thereby."

I can attest to the connection between the two verses.

While the neighbor was the one who was designated to rescue my father, it was in my mother's merit that he was saved. She held out her hand to the poor and extended her hand to the destitute, not closing her door or her heart to the hungry.

In her merit, and only in her merit, her husband's heart could trust in her. The word "heart" takes on a double meaning here.

An Open Check

A young kollel student (and part-time businessman) is handed an open check by a donor who is enthusiastic about him.

This check almost opens doors for him…

But not the doors he hoped for.

He needs a lot of merit to stay out of jail.

They say when wine goes in, secrets come out, but in his case, when the wine went in, the check went out.

My story took place last Purim.

To give you the full picture, I'll try to describe myself, though it's not easy because I wear a lot of different hats.

First and foremost, I learn in *kollel*, but I'm also known in my city for my activities on a communal level. I'm sort of an unpaid activist who's happy to be involved in any Torah-related project. I organize all kinds of activities for children as well as *shiurim* for businessmen and blue-collar workers. *Baruch Hashem*, during Iyar, I organize a full day of Torah lectures for the residents of the city. Actually, I've even invited you, Chaim Walder—twice to speak to parents and once to give an evening presentation to adults in general.

You want to know where all the money's coming from? So it's like this. You can find me in city hall nudging the people who sit on the Torah cultural committee to designate small amounts from their budget to fund all sorts of activities. The rest I raise myself. Some people give money, others donate food and refreshments.

Naturally, everyone knows me, and if you mention my name in my hometown, most people wearing a *kippah* will know who you're talking about. I've made lots of connections and plenty of friendships over the years.

And now for my story.

Last Purim, I went from one shul to another joining their celebrations and hopefully adding some joy as well until finally, I arrived at a shul whose membership is very affluent. I'm purposely leaving it at that and not getting more specific.

I started dancing with them to the sounds of loud music, and I really brought them a spirit of gladness and joy. Everyone was dancing with me. It was *leibedik*.

Suddenly, a man I've known for many years came over to me and said, "Michael, I love you, you're a good person, you're very precious to me."

It's okay. That's how you talk after a few glasses of vodka.

I answered him, "Yes, *achi*, I love you, too."

"I want to give you money," he said, "because you deserve it. You're a good person."

"It's okay, *neshamah*," I told him. "Forget about money now. Let's dance and be happy."

But he pulled out of his pocket an envelope stuffed with cash and checks, fished out a check, and said to me, "Here—this is for you."

I looked at the check, and my eyes lit up. "You're kidding me. You just gave me a check for 4,500 shekels!"

"I'd give you fifty thousand if I had it. You're a tzaddik, learning Torah. You deserve it."

I tried to give him back the check, but he got mad.

I want you to understand that anger. It was like that of a man you'd harmed. A man you'd wounded to the core. It was a look that contained a glint of violence.

"Are you trying to insult me?" he demanded. "I want to give, so I give. What's the matter with you? You'd better take this check before I—"

I took the check before he could tell me before what...and continued to dance.

Purim was over, and one day I looked in my wallet and saw the check.

I considered calling the man to ask him again if he'd really meant to give me so much money, but then I remembered the hurt look he gave me, so I said to myself, *Leave it alone. You're not going to hurt his feelings a second time.*

I deposited the check online. The actual check remained with me.

The check bounced. Of course.

I called the bank. "The check bounced due to lack of funds in the account, correct?" I asked the clerk.

"Not at all," he told me. "Not enough funds is your turf. The story here is quite simple. The check was written for March 1, 2017, and we're already in 2018."

"So what now?" I asked him.

"Contact the person who gave you the check and ask him to write you a new one. Or, he can let the bank know he made a mistake."

The check was from a lawyer I'd never heard of.

I called and told him I had a check of his dated for the previous year.

"Sorry about that," the lawyer said. "It happens. Stop by my office, and I'll replace it."

"It's hard for me to have to drive to another city," I said to him. "How about if you just call the bank to approve it?"

"Okay. Let me check it out."

I give him my phone number, returned the check to my wallet, and promptly forget about it.

A few days went by before I thought about the check again. I called the lawyer, but he didn't answer.

And then I promptly forgot about it again.

About a week and a half later, out of the blue, I got a call from a blocked number.

I usually don't answer blocked numbers, and I recommend that you don't either. But this time, for some reason, my curiosity overcame my usual caution. I took the call and heard the most chilling sentence a person could ever hear.

"This is the fraud unit of the Tel Aviv Police. You need to come in for questioning."

"For what?" I asked.

"Listen, mister, you don't expect me to tell you what for, and you probably already know what for. Just get yourself down here, that's all."

"But I really don't know what for."

"If so, the situation is much worse," the gruff voice answered. "Are you coming, or do I have to send a squad car?"

"I'll come whenever you say."

He told me to be there at ten the next morning.

I've never been as scared in my life.

That night, I tossed and turned and couldn't fall asleep. In the morning, I left the house without saying a word about it to my wife. After an impassioned davening, I drove to the police station.

The investigator who conducted the interview began by asking me, "Tell me something, do you steal checks every day? Is that why you didn't know why we called you down here?"

What?!

"What do you mean by 'steal checks'?" I said. "I'm one of the most honest people in the world."

"Really? Then what's a check from—" he held up a photocopy of the check and read the lawyer's name "—doing in your possession?"

I breathed a sigh of relief.

"What makes you think I stole it?" I asked, now completely at ease. "I can give you the original." I pulled the check from my pocket.

The investigator was momentarily thrown off balance by my self-confidence, but he quickly recovered. "The fact that you have the check doesn't mean you didn't steal it, especially if the person who gave the check claims that he doesn't know you and he never gave you a check."

"That's true. He doesn't know me," I said. "And I don't know him, either. He gave the check to someone else, and that person gave it to me."

"Who did he give it to?"

"Avram."

"Avram what?"

"Avram from the shul."

"That's his last name, "from the shul"?

"No. He has a different last name. I'm just mentioning that I know him from shul."

"Nice. So what's his last name?"

Actually, I had no idea. I saw him about once a week. It was always, "Hey there, Avram. What's up?" "How's everything going, Avram?" I'm not the type who bothers with last names.

"I don't remember his last name."

"Uh-huh," the investigator said. The look on his face said, *Now I've got him*. "And a person whose last name you don't know handed you a check for 4,500 shekels?"

"Yes, it was on Purim."

"As far as I'm concerned, it could be on Pesach," the investigator said. "How about answering the question?"

I didn't know what to tell him. "How about calling him up so he can confirm that he gave it to me."

"Guess what?" the investigator said. "The lawyer called him, and he said he never gave you that check, and he has no idea who you are."

"That's impossible!"

"He made the call in my presence," the investigator said. "We called him from this very office. We didn't know your name, but we gave him the cell phone number you gave the lawyer. He checked his phone, and the number wasn't listed. He said he doesn't think he'd give 4,500 shekels to someone whose phone number he didn't have. What's more, he doesn't remember giving you this check."

"But he did. Call him up, and you'll see that things will work out."

"No problem," the investigator said, and placed the call.

But for some reason, Avram wasn't answering his phone.

He called again and again, but Avram still didn't answer the call.

Then the investigator said to me, "Listen, we're keeping you in custody until we make some progress. I suggest you confess now. If it's a one-time thing, maybe you'll get off easy."

"You can't do this to me!" I protested. "I'm an honest man. This check was given to me."

He gave me a look. "You do realize, don't you, that everything is against you? The check isn't made out to you, you don't know who you got it from, and the guy denies ever giving it to you."

I asked him to try to contact Avram again and tell him my name. "I'm asking you not to arrest me. I'm an honest man, and it will affect me deeply."

He relented and agreed to delay my arrest until he got through to Avram.

I remained in the room for another two hours until finally, Avram answered.

"Hello, this is the police fraud unit," the investigator said, pulling the call on speakerphone.

"Yes, how can I help you?" Avram sounded scared.

"Attorney __________ (he said the lawyer's name) lodged a complaint that a check he gave you wound up in the hands of a person he doesn't know. In our previous conversation, I gave you a cell phone number, and you said you didn't recognize it or the name of the person it belongs to."

"That's right," Avram said. "I have no idea whose number that is. I didn't give anyone the check."

I interrupted. "I think the number listed is my wife's," I said to the investigator, "because she deposited the check online. Give him my number."

The investigator told him my number, and Avram searched his phone for it. "Uh, yeah," I heard him say. "It says Michael from the shul. I know him."

"What's his last name?" the investigator asked.

"Uh, I don't know, but I do know Michael. Everyone knows him. He's a good person."

I breathed a sigh of relief.

Big mistake.

"So now you confirm that you gave it to him?" the investigator asked Avram.

Silence.

"Look, I really admire him, but I don't think I gave him that check. Let me try to think of a reason I might have given it to him, okay?"

"Avram, it's me," I shouted. "Don't you remember? You gave it to me on Purim when we were in the shul, and we danced."

There was a long silence.

"I'm sorry, but no go. I got drunk on Purim, but not so much as to give you a check for 4,500 shekels. Maybe I dropped it, and you found it?"

I begin to cry. "No way, Avram. You *gave* it to me. You told me you loved me and that I was a *ben Torah*, and I tried to refuse it, but you literally forced me to take it."

"I don't remember any of that," Avram said. "Officer, let it go. I don't want to get him in trouble."

"It's not for you to decide," the investigator said. "To begin with, it's not your check, and since you're not the one bringing charges, you can't withdraw them."

"Let it go," Avram said again. "I don't want him to get in trouble. You know what? Get the lawyer on the line. I'll talk to him."

The investigator got the lawyer on the line, and Avram told him, "Listen, Michael's a good guy. I don't know what happened here, but the check I gave him is one you gave me. I'll take care of it. Please withdraw the complaint."

"If that's what you want," the lawyer said, "I'll withdraw all charges. But I'm going to return the check to you, not him. Understand?"

"No problem," Avram said, and the conversation ended.

"You're getting off easy," the investigator told me. "While I'm not closing the case, I won't arrest you. I suggest you think about how a distinguished person like you found yourself in this situation."

"I don't know why I was put into this humiliating situation, but the truth will out," I said. "I truly believe that eventually, the truth will come to light."

"That's one thing we both agree on," the investigator said. "The truth will out." The way he said it left no room for doubt. He meant it would turn out that I was guilty.

I left there a shattered man. I realized that although I wasn't in danger of being arrested, Avram was convinced that I must have "found" the check or stolen it somehow. It occurred to me that his inebriated state at the time must have blocked all memory of the encounter, and now there I was, stuck in the middle of a real mess.

The next few days were not easy ones.

I sensed Avram didn't keep the information to himself but shared it with other people in shul. I wanted to talk to him about it. I like to get things out in the open. But he cut me off.

"Listen," he said, "let's not talk about it. I understand you're in a difficult situation. I'll forgive you, but look where it could have gotten you."

"Don't do me any favors," I said. "I'm ready and willing to go back for questioning and arrest. I *never* took money dishonestly."

He gave me a look that said, "Yeah, tell me all about it," and walked away.

The month of Nissan arrived, and I felt uncomfortable. I'm always the one who organizes *kimcha d'Pischa*, but this year I just wasn't up to it. I felt like I couldn't go around asking people for money because I could imagine what they'd be thinking: "*Kimcha d'Pischa*, huh? Charity collector, huh?"

It was eating me up, and no one in my family knew what I was going through.

Chol hamoed Pesach arrived, and our family went on a trip.

Naturally, we packed the camera to preserve our trip for posterity. And then something happened that usually happens when you take a picture of a rock ten times.

The camera's memory card got full.

We didn't have a spare, so I said, "We'll have to delete the old pictures."

My son took the camera and flipped through the old pictures, and then I heard him say to his brother, "I'm going to erase all the Purim dancing in shul. It's the same every year. Who needs it?"

As soon as I heard "Purim dancing in shul," I lunged for the camera.

"Give it to me," I told my startled kids. "I need to look through the pictures for a minute."

I went back to the first pictures of that Purim. There it was, the end of the Megillah reading, dancing, drinking, more dancing. There I was, giving a speech while everyone else was drinking vodka and whiskey. The video was getting closer to one particular moment in time. Was it recorded or not?

And then, there it was.

The camera moves closer to Avram and me. He's dancing, happy, enjoying himself. He hugs me and says, "Michael, I love you, you're a good person, you're very precious to me."

"Yes, *achi*, I love you, too."

"I want to give you money," he says, "because you deserve it. You're a good person."

"It's okay, *neshamah*," I tell him. "Forget about money now. Let's dance and be happy."

And then he takes out the envelope stuffed with money, pulls out the check, and gives it to me. I protest, and he gets angry with me and says, "I'd give you fifty thousand if I had it."

It continued to the end. I had the proof that cleared my name.

I told the kids, "Sorry, but we can't use this camera anymore." Luckily, there was a cousin with us who also had a camera.

I put ours in a safe place, out of reach and out of sight, as if it were the most priceless possession in the world.

Which it really was. Because it contained the most priceless possession in the world: my good name.

That very same evening, I went to Avram's house and showed him the video.

He was stunned. He apologized profusely and immediately called the lawyer and told him the story.

"Is he there with you now?" the lawyer asked.

"Yes, why?"

"Ah, I see. Everything's okay," the lawyer said, and I realized that he thought Avram just wanted to clear my name.

I decided that I would clear my name myself, to the maximum.

The next day I arrived at the office of the fraud unit and showed the investigator the video. Then I visited the lawyer, and showed it to him. He was convinced, and insisted on writing a letter clearing me of all suspicion and sending it to the investigator.

All that was left was the shul.

I didn't know what to do. Should I show the video to everyone in shul? Maybe they didn't even know anything about the story in the first place.

The person who solved the matter was none other than Avram himself.

On *motza'ei Shabbos*, he told everyone in shul the whole story. He said that because he'd already told the story to several people there, he thought that just as he hadn't been careful about the halachos of *lashon hara*, they probably hadn't been either, so he now wanted to tell them the real story to repair what he had damaged. While he was talking, his son ran home and brought a screen, and Avram played the video for everyone.

Avram announced that he had decided to donate double the amount of the check to a *gemach* I ran and asked everyone there to give as well, to demonstrate their trust in me.

The story was impressive, and everyone contributed generously, so that the end result of this whole story was only good.

That's my story. All's well that ends well.

The moral: "Judge everyone favorably," and "someone on his way to do a mitzvah will come to no harm."

And most important: The truth will out.

Shortcut

The son of the legendary Yerushalmi returns with a hilarious story that could only happen to a Yerushalmi.

Imagine the most dignified, respectable person you know, the one in whose presence you're on your best behavior.

It's taken you six months just to get him to agree to meet you. And when he finally does, everything that can go wrong does go wrong.

The management of "People Speak" takes no responsibility for the health of its readers due to the paroxysms of laughter they may experience while reading this story.

Dear Mr. Chaim Walder,

This is the son of the Yerushalmi writing to you.

Last Purim I heard you give a talk titled "Yerushalmis Speak," and along with my wife, I heard your father as well as Rabbi Abraham Fisher, who's my age and whom I've known personally from the time he made music on water glasses before he found his accordion. For some reason, I never knew your father. Maybe because he didn't make music *even* on water glasses.

What I want to tell you here is about my friend "Sender Schlimazel" of blessed memory. I permit myself to use his nickname because he is no longer with us and so will certainly not take offense, especially because if he didn't take offense when he was alive, he definitely won't take offense after his passing.

You can disparage "Sender Schlimazel" as much as you like, but he was a true friend, and being a "true friend" is something we Yerushalmis value highly. Likewise, I must point out that the nickname Sender Schlimazel doesn't really capture his essence. Not because Sender wasn't a schlimazel. He definitely *was* a schlimazel and a schlemiel, and some would say a *bish gada*, which means "a lost cause" in Aramaic, in case you didn't know. But no matter which way you look at it, he was the luckiest schlimazel in the world.

When we learned with Sender in cheder, we were guaranteed that no harm would come to us from the teachers and administrators who used to dispense *potches* here and there. And that's due to one simple statistic: When you played a prank with Sender Schlimazel nearby, chances are that he would be the one caught and the one to pay the full price for the mischief while his friends fled in a timely manner, and at the most served as guarantors or witnesses or whatever you want to call it and watched as Sender paid in full for their funny business.

If Sender ran away from cheder, you could be sure it happened exactly at the moment the principal arrived. And if

Sender disappeared somewhere for a few hours, you can be sure that exactly then something would happen so that his parents needed him right that very minute. So instead of being able to sneak back in without anyone noticing, the way we all used to do, Sender's disappearance always became a major public event, with concerned parents and uncles and neighbors all asking, "Where's Sender?"

I well remember that when Sender's grandmother was on her deathbed, his father came to the yeshivah (I might be skipping a few years, but there's no chronological order in the Torah) and told Sender outright, "Sender, my son, it's common knowledge that you have a tendency to disappear for a few hours now and then, but I'd like to ask that for the next few weeks you try to stay in the yeshivah or at least within a stone's throw away, for your dear savta's old pump is beating its last, and from the squeaks I'm guessing it won't last more than another week or two. So, please, if you do disappear, stay near enough so that we'll be able to find you without having to mobilize all of Meah Shearim in general and Batei Ungarin in particular."

Sender skipped over the polite words used in such circumstances and said, "Abba, don't talk like that. Savta will live forever." You see, Yerushalmis don't believe that "polite" words can change the functioning of old pumps, certainly not a squeaky pump like that of Sender's grandmother. Yerushalmis believe in traveling to Meron or any other tomb in the north, a combination of prayer and pure pleasure, or as they say in Yiddish, "business with pleasure." He reassured his father that he didn't intend to move further away from the area than you could throw a marshmallow, which is known to not gain momentum and lands very close to where the thrower is standing. (As an aside, I'd like to take this opportunity to protest the younger generation throwing marshmallows instead of candy at the bar mitzvah boy. It's hard to believe the depths to which this generation has sunk. Here in Yerushalayim, we used to throw "*kandel-tziker*," heavy chunks of sugar with sharp points, at the bar mitzvah boy. That's what we had to deal with back then. Then they went down to candy, then to Bambalik, a licorice treat as soft as toffee, but now even toffee has become dangerous for today's pampered youngsters.)

Anyway, after Sender made his father all sorts of promises about his whereabouts at the time of his grandmother's departure, in the yeshivah the betting began, with most boys willing to put everything they had, and maybe even their own grandmother, on the likelihood that Sender would not be in the area at the time of his grandmother's death. Only a very tiny minority were willing to bet on the unlikely possibility that, when the terrible news arrived, Sender would be sitting in the *beis medrash* to receive the news with a heavy heart.

The fact that almost everyone bet the opposite is because of the immutable fact of "Sender's mazel," which is a synonym for "bad luck" or "*bish gada*," or in short: "Sender Schlimazel."

A week went by with Sender trying to stick to the original plan and remain within a certain proximity to the yeshivah. However, it turned out that his grandmother's old pump, known as a heart, managed to last far longer than the repairmen at Bikur Cholim Hospital gave it, even beyond the terms of the warranty. That's how two weeks turned into two and a half weeks, and for Sender, some of the pressure eased up.

So when the news of his grandmother's passing reached the yeshivah, who do you think was missing if not Sender Schlimazel?

The problem was, no one knew or could even guess where he was. It was ten thirty at night. And, as you know, in Yerushalayim, the dead are not left overnight, so now go find Sender Schlimazel.

I was the only one who knew where Sender was. Since it was impossible to say *where* Sender was, as will be explained further on, I picked up my two feet and ran to where I knew Sender could be found.

To where did I run? To a basement being used for baking matzos. Sender was an expert *riedler* (the person who makes the holes in matzah), and since, like the rest of us, he hadn't gotten a cent from his parents since the day he was born or even before that, he found a way to survive by baking matzos, stringing tzitzis, *leining* the Torah, weaving *koishiklach* to hold the *arba minim*, and all the businesses that Yerushalmis are good at.

I reached the basement, walked between the *farnamar* (who mixes the flour and water), the *finerim* (the ones who jump on the dough to roll it), the cutters, and the *katcherim* (who work with the rolling pin), up to the *reidler*, who "coincidentally" or not, was Sender Schlimazel.

"Shalom, Sender," I said to him. "*Kim ahere!* Come with me fast."

"What do you mean come with you?" Sender replied. "Look how much work I have here."

I decide to skip the usual ceremony of "your grandmother wasn't feeling well, so they took her to the hospital and now they're worried that..." It's unnecessary for a Yerushalmi. I cut straight to the chase. "Your savta is *gestorben*."

"Ahhhhh," Sender said, making holes in two more matzos while saying the ahhhhh.

"Come fast, because everyone's waiting at the *beis medrash* asking, 'Where's Sender?'"

That's when Sender realized he had to stop what he was doing and run. He called over a substitute, gave him the hole maker, and ran with me.

Along the way, he passed by one of the *finerim* and told him, "I didn't jump today. Let me jump a little," and he took the rolling pin and jumped on the dough like a rooster. Only when he was finished did he say, "Let's go! *Ya'alah*. To the funeral!"

When we got there, half of Batei Ungarin was waiting at the *beis medrash*. Sender ran ahead fast, and when I saw him running, I realized I had made a mistake by not suggesting that he remove his white hat and apron before arriving at his grandmother's funeral, not to mention dust off the flour stuck to his hair and face.

So actually, Sender Schlimazel's grandmother, who passed away close to Pesach, merited to have a grandson who appeared to be wearing a Purim costume attend her funeral.

Not only did she not laugh, for obvious reasons, but her son laughed even less, for he was none other than Sender's father who had pleaded with his son to make sure to be in the area when the grandmother passed away, yet not only was he not there at the crucial moment but he was also exposed to the whole neighborhood as working as a matzah baker instead of a sitting in yeshivah and learning.

The only reason I'm telling you this whole story is to give your readers a true understanding of Sender Schlimazel, which, in my opinion, paves the way to tell the story I wanted to tell you in the first place.

This story happened around twenty years later when we were both married and had children. Sender Schlimazel, like every Yerushalmi, was busy with all sorts of things: acting as a broker for deals, making tzitzis, selling religious items, baking matzos part of the year, selling the four species at Succos time. Things like that.

One day he told me an opportunity had come his way that could change his life.

As soon as he said it, I knew I had to stop him from going through with the plan, no matter what it was, because as it was, his life wasn't much, and if he changed it, who knew how much worse it might get.

Naturally, I didn't breath a word or even hint at what I was thinking because he might have taken it as an insult or thought I was trying to spoil things. Therefore, I waited for him to tell me.

"You know the Bucharim Hekdesh?" he asked me.

What's the question? Of course I knew it. In a flash, the wheels of my mind started spinning, and I realized all too well the connection between Sender the Schlimazel and the aforementioned Hekdesh.

For the benefit of those who are not Yerushalmis, let me just say that the "Bucharim Hekdesh" is a charitable trust consisting of several buildings whose worth does not exceed one hundred million dollars. The buildings were donated way back when by someone who had no heirs or didn't like them donated the buildings for the public good. However, this so-called "public" is usually not that well-defined, and when it comes to such expensive structures, every "public" wants to define itself as *the* public the man intended.

This Hekdesh, unlike others, was in the hands of several law firms that quarreled with each other over which one of them would have the privilege of *volunteering* to manage it.

And, if you ask yourself, what do law firms have to do with generous bequests, you're not mistaken. It turns out that they pay other people to manage the buildings for a tidy sum, some of which makes its way into the padded pockets of even the least of those law offices.

Yes, Sender Schlimazel probably also wanted to *manage* a *hekdesh* or at least part of one. I'm not judging him for that, either. After all, it's the dream of every Yerushalmi just starting out to want to manage two or three *hekdeshes*. It does away with the need to go abroad to collect money to marry off the children, though I have met several people who seem to feel that there's no shame in doing both, and with all due respect to the money that administrating a *hekdesh* brings in, you can't *neglect* those living in the diaspora who find themselves bitterly disappointed at not having a share in building one of the ruins of Yerushalayim or whatever.

Anyway, it turns out that Sender had been sniffing around the offices of the law firm for a full year and had promised them the world and everything in it and was telling them what he could do with one of the *hekdeshes*, how he could improve the property, and how much better it would be for him to manage that part of the Hekdesh.

"I was finally able to convince them," he told me now, "and tomorrow I have a meeting with one of the partners in the law firm, a fellow named Gerhard Hess, who will accompany me to the property in question."

"Gerhard Hess? That sounds like—"

"Yes, I checked it out. There's no connection to Rudolph the Nazi, may his name and memory be blotted out," Sender declared, and those same wheels spinning in my head announced to me that most likely Sender had *asked* Gerhard if he had anything to do with Rudolf, which certainly couldn't have earned him any points with that same Gerhard. But I didn't say anything, because Sender might take my comment as a criticism.

"What I want from you is to come with me when I take this Gerhard around, because I'll probably feel a bit intimidated by him, and you can help me keep up my end of the conversation if needed and sing my praises, which I refrain from doing out of professional and ethical considerations," said Sender.

When a Yerushalmi friend asks you do to him a favor, you agree. What's more, I had nothing to do that afternoon anyway. So that's how I found myself driving Sender's Ford Cortina, which was as polished as a Yerushalmi can polish his jalopy. We drove to Rechov Yafo to the law firm and waited for Mr. Gerhard to come down. He did just that at the exact time, to the second, that he said he would, because Gerhard Hess, in case you didn't guess from his name, is the most punctual type of Yekkeh there is: Made in Germany.

He approached Sender's battered Cortina, and only because I looked carefully at his face could I detect a slight grimace, for people like him don't know such cars even exist.

Sender hurried to clear off the front seat from the objects cluttering it, and when I say "objects," I mean the contents of a medium-sized apartment in Katamon—clothes, towels, a generator, screwdrivers and a hammer, a few sandwiches, bags of onions, and a small stool of the type you use on Tishah B'Av.

Naturally, I was highly critical of Sender the Schlimazel for not clearing all this stuff off the seat earlier but mostly I found fault with the fact that he *threw* all the above items into the back, *forgetting* the passenger sitting there, who was none other than me, and even with all my friendship with Sender the Schlimazel, I wasn't willing to have objects land on me, especially not that same bag of onions I mentioned earlier and certainly not a hammer with the wrong part aimed at me.

Mostly I was angry at the fact that, unintentionally, Sender was transferring to me the role of the schlimazel and taking for himself the role of a schlemiel who unintentionally throws things at the schlimazel.

"Remember," the Yekkeh informed Sender, "I have only twenty-five minutes to see the property and return."

"Of course I remember," Sender declared, which instantly took my mind back to the way he *remembered* that his grandmother was on her deathbed and that he shouldn't go more than ten minutes away from the yeshivah.

We drove off.

I expected Sender to say little, especially if he wanted to find favor in the eyes of the Yekkeh, sitting like a thorn stuck in our car. But for Sender, it wasn't a day for fulfilling expectations, at least not mine, and so he talked nonstop and told all his personal history, while the Yekkeh sitting beside him said one word repeatedly: "Aha."

When we reached the Bucharim neighborhood, an overly enthusiastic Sender forgot to turn where he was supposed to, a mistake that might cost him a full ten minutes he didn't have, according to the Yekkeh's pronouncement.

He slowed down, and his facial expression showed signs of distress.

And then he came to an open field (nowadays it's packed with buildings, but then it was a broad expanse with no buildings on it). The area bordered the very same building that Sender wanted to manage.

"There it is," said Sender, pointing. "Only a minute away."

And what did Sender do, if not veer off the road and head straight for the open area between the road and the building?

Naturally, I saw this as breaking the rules, but I didn't voice my opinion because Sender was pretending that this was the *only* way to get there.

"If I'm not mistaken, you missed the turn," Gerhard grumbled.

Apparently, he knew all too well how to reach the property.

"Sure, there are those who take a different route, but I know my way around here, and I know the shortest way to get there," Sender babbled, sounding like a municipal department head who had been involved in planning the city's network of streets.

"Aha," Gerhard said, repeating the same aha he'd said earlier but with a note of displeasure.

The car drove about a hundred yards through the open field, and then it hit a sandy patch, and we observed two things at once:

1. The car's engine was running.

2. The car was staying in the same place.

That meant that the wheels were spinning in the sand, trying hard to reach the depths of the earth.

I could see Gerhard's face in the rearview mirror (which was broken, it should be noted), and what I saw was a shadow of worry. Then I looked at Sender's face, and there I saw that the Yekkeh's shadow was only a *reflection* of the worry on Sender's face.

Nonetheless, Sender smiled graciously, as if it was the most normal thing in the world to get stuck with a stuffed-shirt lawyer named Gerhard, a born-and-bred Yekkeh, in a sandstorm with a growling vehicle and wheels spinning in the same place. Actually, they weren't spinning in exactly the same place. It was more like they were sinking deeper and deeper into the soft stuff.

"Let me get out for a sec and see what's going on," Sender offered, and he got out to take stock. I judged from his expression that it was a real disaster.

"We've got a problem here," Sender repeated as if he'd just discovered something we hadn't known. "The car has sunk in the sand up to the doors, so I think it would be best for the two of you to get out for a minute while I try to jump the car forward to get us out of this sandbox quick as a wink."

"I am getting out," Gerhard said in a monotone. He tried to open the door, but, as Sender secretly suspected, the sand piled up against it prevented that.

If awkwardness could kill, they would have found three dead bodies there. However, awkwardness doesn't kill, and certainly not Yerushalmis. Although I must admit that for the first time in my life, I *experienced* that same unfamiliar feeling known as "awkwardness."

"If you get out of the car, it'll rise up a bit, and then we can open your door," Sender suggested, and immediately realized that he had just made a completely illogical suggestion.

"I'll get out," I said, squeezing myself out of the car. Sure enough, the car rose up slightly due to my impressive weight, and the even more impressive lawyer could now open the door and get out.

We stood motionless like two marble statues next to the vehicle. Sender switched gears, and it struck me right then and there that a catastrophe might be headed our way. But before I could get a word out, Sender stepped on the gas, and what happened?

The car didn't budge but due to our departure, which lightened the load, and because Sender frantically turned the steering wheel this way and that, the wheels raised a cloud of sand on all four sides, and within seconds a cloud of dirty sand covered the distinguished lawyer and me from the tips of our shoes to the scalp on our heads.

Sender Schlimazel didn't notice what was happening. He continued to step on the gas and turn the wheel back and forth. He didn't hear us shouting at him to stop, and I must admit that I hadn't expected a fellow like Gerhard Hess to shout. He'd actually seemed like a very quiet person until the sandstorm took direct aim at him from top to bottom.

"*Halten*! *Halten*!" the Yekkeh shouted.

Only then did Sender realize that the two people who'd gotten out of the car had turned into pillars of sand and that one of them was none other than the distinguished lawyer he'd been trying for a whole year to persuade to come with him to the property in question.

He got out. I could see he was a little worried, because, after all, nothing in his life had prepared him for a situation like this, and I can testify that Sender has been through more than a few *situations* in his life.

I looked at the lawyer. It was worse than you can imagine. All sand, he shook his glasses, from which quantities of sand fell, shook his head, upon which grains of sand had landed, and tried to open his eyes but wandered around blindly.

Sender ran to help him and tried to brush off the sand. What a mistake that was! Because Sender, before his failed attempt to move the car, had tried to straighten the tires, which meant his hands looked just like the hands of someone who'd tried to straighten tires manually.

He had removed the sand from the lawyer's face, which was now covered with black tire grease, and as if that wasn't enough, for lack of a nearby mirror, the lawyer had no way of *knowing* that he looked like an African in the Sahara Desert. But we did see it, and at that point, what Yerushalmis do is just burst out laughing.

I looked at Sender, and he looked at me, begging me with his eyes not to laugh. We both bit our lips until blood ran.

But then Sender's hand brushed off the lawyer's white shirt, and according to the results he could see on his shirt, the lawyer drew a quick conclusion as to what the rest of him must look like.

There was a moment of silence, a moment when we were thinking about what we could do right then. I think that was the moment when we realized that the deal would not go through even if the lawyer's life depended on it, and that was exactly what relieved all the tension. We went back to being Yerushalmis from Batei Ungarin and started laughing.

What's laughter? The way we laughed there—like we hadn't laughed in years. We just roared with laughter.

We didn't care about the lawyer or the property we'd lost anyway. Sender and I rolled with laughter. We were doubled over with laughter and laughed as if there was no tomorrow.

The lawyer looked at us—and right then, the skies opened up and rain poured down on us. Before our eyes, the fancy lawyer turned into a walking dirty mop. His pressed suit piled high with sand turned into a mud-filled rag, and for a split second, we wondered what would become of him.

Well, what do you think happened if not that Gerhard Hess, with all his sixty years of being a German, pointed at both of us and started laughing a laugh we'd never heard before.

It wasn't the laugh of a Yerushalmi because Yerushalmis laugh a lot, and their laughter sounds like gravel rolling around. The Yekkeh's laugh was the laugh of one who'd never laughed before. It was a laughter that sounded like heavy rocks rolling around.

"Ha, ha, ha!" the lawyer laughed, and his strange laugh brought on more peals of laughter from us, and as if by coincidence the torrential rain turned into hail, and the three of us laughed like three madmen.

"Let's go on foot," the lawyer suggested, as if he had not, in one moment, been transformed from a polished lawyer into a pile of dirty rags.

We walked all the way to the property, surveyed it as if all the things that had happened earlier were perfectly ordinary, and as if we hadn't just given the professional lawyer a quick lesson in what it means to be a Yerushalmi.

At one point, Sender signaled for me to find a pay phone to

call for help. I slipped away and called Yankel from the *chevra kaddisha*, with all the equipment that lowers the dead to the grave and raises cars from the pit, and the muscular Shloime Zalman, who just leans on a car and it drives off, plus half a dozen Yerushalmi friends who'll come help you at any time and in any situation, even though they have nothing to do anyway, and if they accidentally do have something to do, what won't they do for a fellow Yerushalmi?

And when Sender and the Yekkeh returned to the car, they saw seven Yerushalmis working on the car, tying it to the *chevra kaddisha* van parked nearby, and then with a little push-pull, a few minutes later the vehicle stood on the side of the road.

"Who's this?" Shloime Zalman said, giving a friendly clap on the shoulder to the lawyer, who certainly didn't look like a lawyer right then.

"Him?" Sender said. "He's a friend of ours."

"You already have clean-shaven, modern friends, huh?" Shloime Zalman shouted.

I pinched Shloime Zalman, and he shouted, "What are you pinching me for? What did I say wrong?"

When the guys realized what had happened, Yankel took the lawyer home in the *chevra kaddisha* van where they parted in friendship, and we were all left to laugh with Sender and about Sender, how he once again justified the good name for which he'd toiled many years: Sender Schlimazel.

But then, a few days later Sender got a phone call from the prestigious law firm. Mr. Gerhard Hess informed him that it had been decided to allow him to manage said building while receiving a substantial salary.

And when he arrived at the office, the lawyer told him,

"The truth is, we choose who will manage the properties for us very carefully, but this time I'm deviating from our usual procedure." He coughed slightly to make sure Sender got the meaning of that statement, a sort of hint that this time, the choice was not made with strict adherence to protocol. "Now, all you need to do is sign here and here and here and here," Hess said.

When that was done, the Yekkeh told Sender, "I know what you think about Yekkehs. They say we have no sense of humor. It's not true at all. It's just that our sense of humor is *different* from yours. We view your humor the same way you look at ours, with contempt and condescension. When I was with you this time, it was the first time I connected with your humor."

Then he told him: "And I was impressed by something else. You have good friends, and you seem to know how to get things done. I convinced my partners that this time, we don't need to worry about who will run the business as long as he brings us profits. This building has been sitting for fifty years, and in all that time, it's only accrued debts. We decided that we need someone who can find a shortcut. I think I've found the best person for the job."

Sender shook his hand and turned to leave, but then heard the lawyer say to him, "But I have one condition."

Sender turned around.

"This won't be written in the agreement, and soon you'll realize why. I want your word that none of this will be made known to my partners. I imagine that if they picture what happened there, they will never be able to treat me with the respect and high regard with which we are used to treating each other."

"Done," said Sender.

Fifty years have gone by since then. All those lawyers have

passed away, including Gerhard Hess. And of course, Sender Schlimazel himself. So, since the prohibition is no longer in effect due to the passage of time and the fact that the statute of limitations has expired, I gave myself permission to tell you this story, Mr. Walder, which shows how Yerushalmi simplicity can sometimes take a shortcut and win.

"...Until You Have Mercy on Your Children"

They're on their way home from making a chalakah in Meron when they find themselves in the scariest place in the world.

Just when they think it's all over, they discover their nightmare has yet to begin.

If you think it can't happen, think twice.

We're a family of five, and we live in Modi'in Illit.

Our story took place on Lag BaOmer 5777/2017. Aside from it being a dramatic story, I see a real obligation to publish it. It appeared in the general press at the time, but without its important spiritual messages.

Lag BaOmer that year began on *motza'ei Shabbos*. We planned to make a *chalakah* (what some call an *upsheren*) for our son, Evyatar.

My husband was adamant about not contributing to the Shabbos desecration caused by security preparations for the *motza'ei Shabbos* crowd, so we decided to leave for Tiveria on

Thursday and spend Shabbos in Tiveria with our parents and my husband's brother, who was also making a *chalakah* for his son. The plan was to drive to Meron only on Sunday.

On Shabbos, we made a birthday party for the two boys. *Motza'ei Shabbos,* we made a bonfire in Tiveria, and on Sunday morning we drove to Meron, leaving the car in Chatzor and taking a shuttle to the tomb of Rabbi Shimon.

We davened, made the boys their *chalakah*, then davened some more and spent the rest of the day there.

In the evening, we returned by shuttle to Chatzor, where we'd left our car. We visited the tomb of Choni Hame'agel nearby and davened there.

I remember my attention being drawn to the words that Choni uttered when he prayed for rain. He drew a circle around himself and prayed to Hashem, "I swear by Your Great Name that I will not move from here until You have mercy on Your children." Although the prayer was part of a plea for rain, something about the words "have mercy on Your children" moved me. I had no idea of the personal meaning those words would assume in just a few hours.

From Chatzor, we drove back to Tiveria, packed up, and said our goodbyes.

We set off for home. As we were driving, my husband stopped abruptly, got out of the car, and walked back to his brother's car, which was right behind us. Handing his brother a few shekels, he said, "Be our *shaliach* for a mitzvah, and you won't be harmed."

Neither of them knew how prescient those words were.

We turned on the GPS, typed in "Modi'in Illit," and continued our journey.

Miles later, out of the blue, one of the children said to us, "I don't know what to do. I feel so scared."

Actually, I felt the same way. I had a kind of vague feeling of unease, a dread of unknown calamity about to take place. But even my imagination couldn't prepare me for what actually did happen on this trip.

I heard my husband answer our son, saying, "I feel that way, too, but Hashem is protecting us. Let's all say some *tehillim*."

We said a few *tehillim* together. The car drove on through the dark, but I was wide awake, not asleep as I usually was on long trips, as if my being awake could change anything.

For some reason, the GPS had us take all kinds of strange, unlit routes. My husband explained to me that half the country had gone to Meron (and let me take this opportunity to inform everyone that during the day twice as many people go to Meron as during the night). Now everyone was returning home, so the GPS was giving us alternate routes that weren't as crowded so that we'd get home faster.

Still, my husband had his doubts, and so he rebooted the device. But the GPS repeatedly directed us to the same winding roads until, at some point, the voice announced that we would reach our destination in twenty minutes.

Just then, my brother-in-law called. "Where are you guys? Is everything okay?"

We told him that we'd be home in about twenty minutes and that everything was okay.

Those were the twenty minutes that changed the whole story.

The GPS told us to turn left.

We looked to where it was directing us and saw a very steep ascent. It wasn't even a highway but a dirt road. It seemed very strange to my husband, so he said, "I'll continue straight on ahead."

We drove straight ahead, but the GPS didn't like it and announced: "Recalculating route. Make a U-turn and then turn right."

We saw that it was insisting we take the dirt road, so we decided to follow the instructions.

We turned onto the road. There were no signs. We kept on driving until suddenly it dawned on us that we were in an Arab area. But then again, so what? We were used to it. It had been like that the whole trip, but it didn't make us nervous because sometimes the shortcuts the GPS gives you will take you through a nonhostile Arab village.

But after fifteen minutes of having us wander around a completely unmarked area, the GPS conked out on us.

We had no reception.

Interestingly, it was only after the GPS stopped working that we began to use our brains and realized that something might have gone wrong. Another point for consideration.

We realized that we'd been in an Arab region for fifteen minutes already. It was starting to feel a little like we might even be in Palestinian Authority territory. We called the police and told them we had a feeling we were in trouble.

"Look for a sign and tell me what it says," the policeman instructed us.

There were signs, but only in Arabic.

"Take a picture and send it to us," he said.

"We have a kosher phone," we told him. "What should we do?"

"What's your license plate number?"

Our calls were repeatedly disconnected, which the officer said was a bad sign. "Make sure your cell phones are charged, and your tank is full," he warned.

As if we could.

The children began waking up and asking questions. We said we didn't know where we were and that we were in contact with the police.

When they heard "police," they panicked. Now, besides our own nervousness, we had to deal with the children's anxiety as well.

Just as we'd adjusted to our fearful state, we noticed that we had escorts.

Ten vehicles emerged from all kinds of holes, clearly not by accident. They surrounded us. Two cars drove ahead of us and blocked our way. As in the worst nightmare, there we were inside the Palestinian Authority, trapped on all sides.

People started pouring out of the cars and then out of the surrounding houses: teens and young men and children. Within two minutes, we were surrounded by hundreds of people, and still more kept coming.

Then came the banging on the car. Hard pounding that took our breath away as they beat on the hood, the roof, the doors, the windows. We were terrified and had no idea what to do.

We called the police and screamed, "We're surrounded by hundreds of Arabs! They're rocking the car and banging on it!"

"Where are you? Where are you?" shouted the policeman, and we sensed that he was even more nervous than we were.

"How should we know?" I cried out, sobbing. "There are thousands of Arabs here! They're going to kill us!"

It was a mistake to say that in front of the children, but who could think straight right then? Besides, our kids were smart enough to realize on their own the kind of situation we were in.

"Hello? Hello?" The call was cut off yet again.

Outside, we saw an Arab walking through the crowd. His authoritative presence caused the crowd to part before him. Suddenly, there was a leader of all this mob.

We didn't know if it was good or bad. In those moments, it seemed that anything might be better than an out-of-control mob with murder in their eyes.

I called the police again. "Tell us what to do! In another few minutes, it will be too late!"

I heard the policeman say to someone, "*Oy vavoy*. They're surrounded. We've got to do something."

That was the moment when I realized that the police couldn't help us. It was Hashem and only Hashem Who could help us.

I whispered, "Shema Yisrael, Hashem, please help me," and suddenly, the words of Choni Hame'agel popped into my mind: "I will not move from here until You have mercy on Your children." I said it over and over, desperately.

The Arab who'd taken charge shouted to my husband, "Open the window!"

That was the hardest moment of all.

What should we do? Should we open it?

"Don't open it!" I hissed.

"But maybe he's trying to get things under control," my husband said. "I'll open it a crack and talk to him."

The pounding on the car became unbearable, I couldn't understand how the windows still held. It was obvious that it was only a matter of seconds before they'd break in, and then...

That's when I realized that everything was out of control and that maybe this Arab was the only one who could somehow take charge of the situation.

We saw that he was trying to calm the mob, and at the same time gesturing forcefully to us to open the window.

My husband decided to open it.

"Give me the cell phone," the Arab commanded my husband. He said the words *cell phone* in Arabic.

My husband hesitated.

Meanwhile, I surreptitiously pressed Send to the police phone, without putting the phone to my ear.

He took my husband's phone and said to me, "Give me belephon." (He meant "*pelephone*," which is Hebrew for cell phone, but there is no "p" sound in Arabic.)

My cell phone was our only connection to the outside world.

"Hand it over," he demanded.

Something about him evoked fear. Still, he obviously controlled the scene, and what endangered us was lack of control, because the crowd seemed bloodthirsty.

It was pretty clear to us that if he were to leave, the crowd would rip us to shreds.

My gut feeling said we had no choice but to go along with this, even though it looked like a huge mistake, giving him our only connection to the outside world.

He took my cell phone, put it in his pocket, and shouted something in Arabic to the mob. He was evidently an authority. He got into his car, which blocked us from the front, and motioned us to follow.

My husband didn't move. "Who knows where he wants to take us?" he said.

The Arab motioned to us to get a move on.

We realized we had no choice. Staying where we were meant certain death. There—wherever "there" was—they might keep us captive and maybe kill us, but it was still a delayed sentence, so we went for it.

We started driving after him, with the mob still banging on the car and running alongside us. The car in front of us gradually picked up speed, and so did we. The mob chased after us throwing stones. After a minute, the only thing following us were the cars, making sure we didn't escape.

We entered a place that looked like a city, drove a few more minutes, and then reached a gate.

"Oh no!" my husband cried. "*No, no, no...*"

"What's the matter?"

He didn't respond.

"What happened? Talk to me!"

"I recognize this place," he said. "It's the police station in Ramallah."

"How do you know? Were you ever here?"

"I wasn't here, but I know," he said.

Then I realized how he knew.

Seventeen years earlier, two IDF reservists, Yossi Avrahami of Petach Tikvah and Vadim Nurzhitz of Or Akiva, were traveling in a private vehicle on Route 443. They made a mistake, and instead of continuing to the Hizma checkpoint and bypassing Ramallah, they continued straight toward the city. Exactly the same thing that happened to us.

When they reached a Palestinian Authority roadblock, they were detained by policemen and taken to the local police station. An angry mob heard about the Jews being detained and began throwing stones at the compound and rioting.

The news of soldiers being captured in Ramallah was received by the army within fifteen minutes, but the IDF decided that a rescue operation would be too dangerous because of the expected resistance of Palestinian security forces, who are well trained in their city's urban area.

Avrahami and Nurzhitz didn't stand a chance. The inflamed mob stormed the police station and slaughtered them. The mutilated body of Nurzhitz was thrown out of the second-story window, and that of Avrahami was dragged out the door to the raging rioters, who stabbed, trampled, and beat him. The Palestinian mob dragged the two bodies down the street to Al Manara Square in the heart of Ramallah—exactly where we were!—and continued to abuse them. They tore their bodies apart, and Norwich's body caught fire. There are other descriptions I'd rather not repeat.

And here we were, right in the very same awful place. Now that we both realized where we were, we withdrew into silence. We didn't say anything to the children, but we realized that we were doomed. Our fate was sealed, and all we could do was trust in our Father in Heaven.

I was crying tears of desperation. "I will not move from here until You have mercy," I murmured over and over again through my tears.

He stopped. A number of people were there waiting for us and told my husband to get out of the vehicle.

My husband got out of the car. His face was as white as chalk. The kids and I were still inside the car, trembling with fear and crying.

They surrounded my husband and motioned him to give them his ID.

My husband gave them his Israeli ID.

They came over to the car and motioned for me to hand over mine.

I told them I didn't have one.

They insisted, and then I "remembered" that my ID was in my wallet, which was in a suitcase.

"Bring it," they said.

I said I didn't know where it was. I did everything I could to stall for time, all the while thinking that the open line to the police hadn't been cut off and that the policeman knew the trouble we were in.

When they saw I wasn't giving it to them, they began opening all the suitcases.

The children were quiet. In shock.

They found my ID. At least I had gained another five minutes of life.

Then we were all ordered to get out of the car.

I felt deeply how I imagined the Jews must have felt during the Holocaust when they faced an *aktion*, were herded into a train, and forced to enter the gas chambers. If until now I hadn't understood their submissiveness, now I understood it all too well.

They took us upstairs to headquarters. Their eyes burned with hostility. They were the strong ones, the ones in command. There was no way we could resist them. We had no weapons. We didn't even have a cell phone.

Again the feeling gripped me that it was only us and Hashem. There was no one we could rely on but Him.

In the room sat a commander who looked like Hitler. He was tough. Scary. Around him were soldiers with drawn weapons, their eyes blazing with hatred. They motioned for us to sit. The children sat, and we stood. The picture of Chanah and her seven sons flashed through my mind, along with all its meaning.

One soldier sat in front of us, smoking a cigarette. He blew the smoke directly into our son Uriel's eyes. He did it deliberately, at a distance of one inch from his face. They all laughed a burst of satanic laughter.

Here's where it starts, I said to myself, thinking of Avrahami and Nurzhitz. I was too terrified to cry.

And then...one of the soldiers put a gun to Uriel's head.

"*Noooo!*" we screamed

He pulled the trigger.

We screamed.

We heard a click. The gun wasn't loaded.

All the soldiers laughed. It was the most wicked laugh I've ever heard.

At that point, we just cried in horror. We were in the lowest place imaginable.

He waved his gun and said, "Tell your soldiers not to kill our children."

He didn't realize that what he'd just said contained a hidden message that gave us hope.

The hatred was there in the air. If hatred could kill, we would have been dead. And if fear could kill, we would have melted in terror.

I said to my husband, "I can't take this."

The soldiers began to speak in Arabic. Because my parents were Moroccan, I understood parts of sentences and grasped more from their hand motions.

We sat there for at least an hour, and all the time, there were soldiers coming in and out and shouting. We understood that they wanted our blood. The original group was trying to calm them down. This must have been what the two soldiers felt before the horrific lynching.

Then an officer came in and said something. It took us a few seconds to realize that he was speaking in Hebrew. He told us, "Come with me."

He handed us our IDs and pointed at us to get in a commercial vehicle. We hesitated, but we had no choice.

We got in the car, and then he handed us our cell phones.

As I was being handed my phone, it rang.

The policeman was on the line.

"What's going on?" he asked. "Where are you?"

"We're getting into a car. They're taking us out of here," I said.

"Don't get into someone else's car!" he shouted.

"We're already in it, and it's moving," I said. "What should we do now?"

"Stay on the line with us," he said, "and describe what you see."

I told him what I was seeing, and after a few minutes, he said, "It's okay. You're heading out."

I stayed on the line, and after twenty minutes that seemed like forever, we reached the checkpoint.

And only then did we realize what a commotion our disappearance had caused.

There were dozens of ambulances, patrol cars, military vehicles, and lots of soldiers. We found out that an entire battalion was preparing to enter Ramallah.

A senior officer welcomed us. He was obviously very

nervous. "You've just experienced a miracle," he said. "We already received the command to go in. We didn't want another lynching. If you hadn't answered that phone call, you have no idea what would have taken place. Chances are you wouldn't have come out of this mess alive."

A few minutes later, someone brought us our car. He said something in Arabic to the officer, who translated. "He says he gave you water."

We confirmed that he was telling the truth and told him "*Shukran*." He said goodbye to us, pleased that we had praised him.

We found out that the only way they could trace us was through our car. They knew exactly where we were, and they also heard that call I made, when the Arab policeman told us to climb the stairs to headquarters. But when the connection got cut off, that alarmed the military authorities, and they gave orders to storm into Ramallah to rescue us.

We drove home. The children were hysterical, and we couldn't stop crying either. We told them, "*Hodu LaShem ki tov*, we were saved by a miracle." We got home and fell onto our beds, dead tired but totally alive.

First thing in the morning the phones began ringing. Every media outlet wanted to interview us and get our story. It was important for me to give public thanks for the miracle. I asked a Rav, and he said it might be beneficial to share the story.

I talked and said everything we had to say, but, of course, the media praised the Arabs as righteous among the nations for releasing us unscathed and downplayed all the descriptions of hatred and threats with the gun. What bothered me the most, though, was the way this discounted all my words of gratitude to Hashem and Rabbi Shimon bar Yochai, and the prayer of Choni Hame'agel.

Now I want to close the circle and tell the whole story as it was, including thanks to the Creator of the World Who bestowed upon us all good, and to Rabbi Shimon Hatzaddik, whose *zechus* stands by us, and of course, to end with the prayer of Choni Hame'agel: "I will not move from here until You have mercy on Your children."

This Doctor Is Always On Call

Erez Farber, a wealthy businessman, took a trip to India.

Riding his motorcycle in one of the most remote regions of the world, he fell into an abyss and landed on his head.

What are the chances of survival for a mortally wounded man who's at the ends of the earth, about as far from a doctor as can be?

Then again...perhaps he was as close as could be to the Healer of all flesh.

Every year, the five Farber brothers took a trip together.

Erez Farber, a resident of Givat Shmuel near Bnei Brak, a wealthy man, the owner of an employment agency for foreign home health aides, was the eldest brother, and he's the main protagonist of our story.

In 2017, the brothers planned a unique vacation to the Indian Himalayas. It was a trip they'd been planning for a long time because of its complexity. No one, however, imagined how complex the trip would actually be.

The Himalayas are the tallest mountains on earth—with narrow trails and breathtaking views that sometimes seem to make people do things that are also truly breathtaking. Permanently.

They took five motorcycles with them. Four of the brothers were experienced cyclists. Erez less so. How much less? He got his license a few short weeks before the trip.

His wife asked him not to ride a motorcycle, but she might as well have asked him not to go on the trip.

"At least make sure you wear a full face helmet," she said.

"I promise," he told her.

She asked that he keep his promise, and he promised to do so.

When the brothers arrived in India, all their equipment had arrived intact, except for—you guessed it—the helmets. They bought half helmets locally. The price was a bargain, but Erez reminded them of his promise to his wife.

"Okay, but it didn't work out. Let it go."

"But I promised."

After a brief discussion, one of the brothers ran to buy Erez a full face helmet. As he handed to it Erez, he said, shaking his head in disbelief at his brother's obstinacy, "Here's your full helmet."

They rode off. Three brothers took the lead, followed by Erez and another brother behind him.

They rode the narrow, dangerous trails of the Himalayas, breathing deeply of the clean air and taking in the spectacular scenery.

As the last brother rounded a turn, he discovered that Erez wasn't in front of him.

He braked his motorcycle sharply and caught a glimpse of Erez plunging over the side of the cliff on his bike.

The other brothers? They were still riding on ahead, unaware of what had just taken place.

Then they got a phone call.

"Come back fast!" their brother shouted.

"What now?"

"Erez fell off the cliff. I don't see how he could have survived."

They raced back and discovered two horrendous things: one, their brother had crashed thirty yards below, the height of a ten-story building, and two, there was no apparent way to reach him.

One of the brothers grabbed on to a pipe snaking down the mountainside and slid all the way down to the middle of the crevasse. Then, he somehow made his way down to his brother lying motionless below. From there, he saw an alternate path down the mountain and directed his other brothers to it.

They quickly reached the place where Erez had fallen and saw him lying there unmoving. They were at a loss. Was he alive? What that even a possibility? But if he was, what should they do? The slightest move might kill him.

They decided to call his wife, Yaffa.

Yaffa's phone rang. Caller ID showed one of her brothers-in-law. She had a feeling it was bad news and decided not to take the call. How did she know? Call it wifely intuition.

Her daughter answered the phone instead, and after a minute, screamed, "Ima, Abba is seriously injured! He's going to die!"

After speaking with her brothers-in-law, Yaffa called the Foreign Ministry and Erez's travel insurance company, PassportCard.

Erez's brothers called again. They wanted to know if she'd made contact with the insurance company.

"Get a helicopter over there!" Yaffa screamed.

"There's no way can we bring a helicopter here until we have a doctor's authorization to move him," the brothers told her.

Hesitantly, they touched Erez. He was still alive, but how much longer could he hold out?

All of a sudden, they saw hundreds of Indians descending the mountain. They hadn't noticed them before this and had no idea what they were doing there.

Just then, a car drove up, and its passengers pulled out an improvised stretcher.

They threw down the stretcher and then slid down the metal pipe all the way down to where the brothers were. The others got down by going around the crevasse.

It was very cold, which made it impossible to remove the injured man's clothing to see the extent of his injuries.

They decided to ease him onto the stretcher, knowing full well that doing so might actually cause his death no matter how careful they were. But leaving him there on the Himalayan mountainside would mean certain death. Faced with a choice between possible death and certain death, they chose the better option of the two.

Erez was carefully carried up the mountain, unconscious and unresponsive, obviously very seriously injured.

The brothers boarded the van in which Erez was placed and immediately tried contacting anyone who might be able to help. The foreign ministry operates a situation room for just such emergencies, but no airline was willing to fly Erez in his current condition.

They drove for three hours in the van, on dirt and gravel roads that shook their critically injured passenger, until they finally arrived at a clinic. But what a clinic! Remember, they were in India. The clinic looked more like a slaughterhouse from a hundred years ago.

The doctors, or whatever they were, were in the middle of examining the patient when they suddenly remembered that they weren't actually doctors and that their usual job consisted of smiling and putting on a bandage.

"There's nothing we can do," they told the brothers. "You'll have to take him to the hospital in Rishikesh. That's a four-hour drive from here."

Erez was again placed on a stretcher and loaded into the van. He struggled to breathe and was still unconscious.

Yaffa called every few minutes. Each time the brothers told her, "You're got to arrange for a helicopter."

Yaffa asked them to put the phone on speaker. The whole way to the hospital, she and their daughters were shouting, "Abba! Abba!" hoping that maybe Erez would hear them and be roused to fight for his life.

"He's struggling for each breath," the brothers told Yaffa, "and we don't know what to do for him. We're losing him."

Yaffa called Rabbis Elimelech Firer and Benny Fisher, who alerted the top doctors in Israel and filled them in on the details. The deputy director of Tel Hashomer Hospital even came to Yaffa's house in Givat Shmuel to talk to the medical staff in India from there.

Night fell. The news spread through the neighborhood. Everyone said *tehillim* and cried. The house turned into a command center. Yaffa called illustrious rabbeim and asked them to pray. The air crackled with tension.

"Get on a plane and fly there," Rabbi Fisher told her.

Meanwhile, the brothers, still on their way to the hospital, were begging for help.

Yaffa called the CEO of the insurance company and said, "I'm ready to sign anything you want. Just get a helicopter over there to take him to a hospital."

The CEO told her that without a doctor's consent, they couldn't authorize it. They were afraid that with punctured lungs, the flight might kill him.

Either way, after a grueling drive of seven hours in total, the brothers arrived with Erez at the hospital in Rishikesh. There, at least, there were X-ray machines. The fuzzy images were like from the 1960s, but at least they were X-rays.

Meanwhile, Yaffa bought tickets for herself and her English-speaking son-in-law and got ready to fly over. At 1:00 a.m., they hit a snag: neither of them had a visa for India.

Kindhearted community activists contacted the Indian ambassador, who issued two handwritten visas in the middle of the night. Yaffa and her son-in-law were able to board their flight.

Erez must have had a lot of mitzvos to his credit, both as an individual and as owner and manager of an employment agency for foreign home health aides. At moments like this, a person's good deeds come back to him. Anyone and everyone who could, extended their hand to help.

At the airport, Yaffa managed to convince Erez's brothers to bribe the doctors in Rishikesh to let them fly Erez by air ambulance (in this case, a helicopter) to New Delhi. Only there did they have a hospital equipped to treat his serious injuries.

Meanwhile, she made arrangements with the hospital in New Delhi and received their assurance that they were ready to receive her husband.

After sneaking Erez out of the hospital, the brothers set out for New Delhi, about 150 miles away, by helicopter. And remember, this is after seven hours of driving with an unconscious, critically wounded man with a serious head injury and a shattered body, with the extent of the damage still unknown.

While they were on their way, Yaffa landed in New Delhi.

It was November 8, 2016. Of all days, it was the last day that it would pay to land in India. That was the day when 500- and 1,000-rupee notes were taken out of circulation. Indian Prime Minister Narendra Modi said in a broadcast throughout India that at midnight, banknotes of those denominations would become "worthless pieces of paper."

Yaffa landed and discovered that she couldn't change her money at the airport money changers because they had no cash. One of the brothers drove to the airport to bring Yaffa to the hospital.

The hospital was like Noah's Ark.

The lower floors were for the masses, where people, chickens, and goats slept side by side. Strong odors pervaded—and they weren't like those of a regular hospital, either. India.

The upper floors were like a magnificent palace. VIP accommodations, with every Western luxury.

All this in the same building.

Yaffa walked into the intensive care unit and saw her husband lying there, in an induced coma and on a ventilator, hooked up to a maze of tubing.

Now it was possible to summarize his condition: he had a

head injury, whose severity had yet to be determined; his skull was cracked in several places; every single rib was broken—some in two places; both arms and both legs were broken; and most serious of all, he had a crack in the neck vertebra. Even the slightest movement could have killed Erez or turned him into a paraplegic for life. And Erez had experienced more than one jolt over the past twelve hours.

The worst injury was the head injury. When a person falls from such a height, he falls on his head, because the head is the heaviest part of the upper body. Erez landed on the helmet (the full face helmet, if you will recall). Although *b'chasdei Shamayim* it prevented his immediate death, the blow to his head and the pressure on his neck were enough to cause serious injury.

Meanwhile, Givat Shmuel mobilized for a series of prayer rallies. People set up shifts throughout the day to say *tehillim* and pray for Erez's recovery.

The unconscious Erez was still on a ventilator and in an induced coma.

At a certain point, Yaffa told the Indian doctors (as she was advised to do by the experts in Israel), "Let's start reducing the sedation so that we can wean him off of it."

It usually takes twelve hours before the patient wakes up.

Yet here, twelve, twenty-four, thirty-six, and seventy hours had passed, but Erez still hadn't woken up.

The doctors were grim. "We're losing him," they said. "He needs a blood transfusion."

But the Israeli team of doctors warned against it. "Don't let them give him a blood transfusion in India."

Reality won. Yaffa was forced to sign her consent to a blood transfusion. The doctors warned her that without it, he'd die.

Yaffa sat by her husband's side from six in the morning to eleven at night. Everyone else took turns.

Yaffa sang Erez all his favorite songs and had him listen to their granddaughters call out to him over the phone, "Saba Erez! Saba Erez!" until the Indian doctors begin to call him "Saba Erez" too.

Yaffa talked to him, but Erez showed no response.

They flew in Dr. Ami Mayo, then head of the Intensive Care Unit at Rambam Medical Center in Haifa. The wife of the Israeli military attaché in India brought food and took care of their laundry.

In the beds next to him, people were constantly dying, and in terrible ways.

But Erez survived, though he was still unconscious.

"We've got to get him out of here," the doctor said. "Otherwise, he'll get pneumonia." But as long as Erez hadn't regained consciousness, he couldn't be flown to Israel.

Yaffa recalled a song Erez used to like: "Though I walk through the valley of the shadow of death." She sang it to him: "I will fear no evil for You are with me."

She sat there singing to him for hours and then—seventy-two hours after the accident—Erez was humming along with her. He was humming off-key, but it was the most beautiful sound she'd ever heard.

Everyone there was crying. In Israel, everyone who knew Erez and heard that he'd woken up after so much time and so many prayers was crying, too.

As soon as Erez woke up, plans to transport him to Israel

shifted into high gear. It was an extremely complex and costly mission.

An ambulance helicopter to the airport brought him right up to the plane, a connecting flight to Istanbul was secured and from there a plane to Israel. A dozen seats had to be removed from each plane to make room for the stretcher.

PassportCard paid for everything. The travel insurance company met their obligation to pay whatever it took—which was a lot—to save Erez's life.

The flight was far from the best thing for him. Perforated lungs and high altitudes don't go well together. No one told Yaffa that only a month earlier someone had died on just such a flight due to similar circumstances.

The flight made Erez's condition worse.

In Israel, people gathered to pray for him and say *tehillim*. Erez's children made sure that one of them woke up every half hour to join the *tehillim* marathon. During the fifteen hours of travel, Erez was surrounded by *tehillim*.

In Israel, doctors waited at the airport, ready to whisk him away to the trauma unit at Tel Hashomer hospital.

The Rachashei Lev association gave the Farber family apartments near the hospital, and from then on, they began taking turns living at the hospital.

And then…Erez caught pneumonia. His fever rose, the doctors were worried to the point of despair. But not Yaffa and the children. More prayers were said, and more appeals were made to the rabbis to beseech Hashem for Heavenly intervention.

After three days, Erez began to recover.

He woke up for the second time, and this is where the family entered a new phase.

Apparently, while he was unconscious, Erez must have

attended Oxford University, because when he woke up, he spoke the Queen's English.

Like an 18th-century English lord, he spoke a fluent high-level English. The family went along with this historical touch until doctors forbade them to speak English with him. The family then made a point of speaking only in Hebrew, and Erez went along with it. But there's another twist to the story.

Erez asked Yaffa, "Who are you?"

"Who am I?" Yaffa said in mock offense. "I'm the cleaning lady. Erez, are you okay? I'm Yaffa, your wife."

Erez pointed to her cell phone and asked, "What's that?"

Yaffa's face fell.

"Who are you?" she asked her husband. "What's your name?"

"I don't know," he replied.

Erez's mental hard disk had been erased.

Erez didn't know how to dress himself. He was as helpless as a newborn baby, which, at his age, presented a very difficult situation.

He began an arduous rehabilitation process, which started with his family showing him pictures of his wife, children, and grandchildren as they told him their names.

Chanukah approached. It was the saddest Chanukah they'd ever had. Yaffa realized that her husband's body might be alive, but what about his soul? Was there a person inside that suffering body?

His daughter Hila was sitting next to him when suddenly, Erez woke up.

For the three hundredth time, she asked him, "Abba, do you know who I am?"

"Hila," Erez replied automatically. "Why are you asking?" He spoke as if it was the most natural thing in the world. He didn't understand why Hila burst out crying and ran to call the rest of the family.

To be eligible for rehab, Erez had to answer thirteen questions. That's all. Things like, "What's your name?" "What's your ID number?" Address, phone number, and more.

Erez didn't know the answer to a single question.

He was injured at the end of 2016 and was stuck there. He had no idea they were in 2017.

He remembered nothing and had no idea where he was. Each time he was asked, he gave a different answer. His age also changed from time to time, though twenty-six was his favorite answer.

Family members begin a process of training him, as part of the recovery efforts.

They didn't believe what was happening: This strong man, owner of a successful business, couldn't even answer thirteen questions, most of which any five-year-old could answer and all of which any second grader could answer. The family suddenly understood what most people never do, which is that we need to thank Hashem every single minute of the day. They also realized the deep truth to the blessing we murmur three times a day: "Who bestows knowledge."

It took Erez almost a month before he could answer all the questions, and on the day he did, everyone celebrated as if he'd just earned his doctorate.

Erez could now enter a rehabilitation program. In addition to speech therapy, he was taught how to eat, stand, and walk.

He spent three months in the hospital, surrounded by his family, who dropped everything to be there for him.

They trained him to read one line at a time and then to remember what he'd read. At first, he couldn't remember anything, but he slowly learned to do so.

Some people take a year to go through this process. Erez did it in three months.

When did his family know he'd gotten back to himself?

When he started doing charitable deeds for others.

There was a rabbi in rehab who'd suffered a stroke and was depressed about his situation. Erez sought him out and gave him tips on how to get through it. There was a child who'd suffered a stroke, and Erez gave him encouragement. To a woman and her daughter, who had suffered a severe stroke, Erez offered reassurance that the daughter would succeed in recovering just as he had done. There was a girl who'd suffered a traumatic brain injury in India that he helped, and when a child from a religious family was injured in an accident, Erez encouraged the devastated father to have hope, and his son did recover.

Erez became a role model in the hospital.

On *erev Shabbos*, the men went to the hospital shul while Yaffa and the girls made *kabbalas Shabbos* with the women. And in the Farber *kabbalas Shabbos*, there were no ethnic groups or communities. They all gathered together and sang *zemiros* together. You could even find Arab women joining them on occasion.

On March 23, Erez was released from the hospital, walked on his own two feet to the car waiting for him, arrived at his home, and there, as usual, took in one bound the three steps from the street to the path leading to the front door.

Erez had come home.

* * *

Thank you to Erez and Yaffa Farber, who hosted me in their home and spent three hours telling me this incredible story. Their sole purpose was to publicly thank the Creator of the world for His many kindnesses to them.

The Arbiter

When there's a dispute between Jews, they go to beis din. Before the hearings begin, they sign a binding arbitration agreement.

Not everyone knows what an arbitration agreement means. It can be more binding than a court ruling, because the arbiter's authority is unlimited, and he doesn't have to explain his reasoning.

Most arbitrators deserve their respected status, but if you meet up with one who doesn't, you can find yourself messed up for the rest of your life.

Unless...

Unless you do such a good deed that Hashem wants to save you from the decree you brought upon yourself.

I think everyone will be touched by my story with its life-altering Divine providence and strong takeaway message.

I learn in *kollel* and am the father of eight children. I live frugally, but I have no complaints.

I'm blessed with a good wife, *baruch Hashem*, who makes no demands. Her sole aspiration is for me to sit and learn. That's her whole world, and to that goal she devotes her whole life.

You don't want to know how a family of ten lives on the wife's monthly salary of 4,000 shekels, the *kollel* stipend of 2,500 shekels, and a few hundred shekels from government child allowances. How did a fellow *kollel* member with six children put it? "When the first child was born, I wondered how I would marry her off, and I had no answer. Now, after the sixth child, I still don't have an answer—but I no longer ask the question."

This may come as a surprise, but not only do I finish the month without any overdraft whatsoever (something hundreds of thousands of working people can't say about themselves), I've even been able to save. I put away a little here and a little there with one goal in mind: to buy a piece of property that I'll later be able to sell at a profit to pay for marrying off two or three children.

As an aside, let me just say that there's a perfectly logical explanation for how *avreichim* can live without an overdraft. It's because they don't waste money.

A car, restaurants, brand-name clothing, travel, vacations—these are all very expensive items. Working people permit themselves all these and more and always find that their expenses are greater than their income.

But when you're spending only on food and simple clothing, especially when you buy the cheapest (you wouldn't believe the difference in price between a standard item of clothing and the same item in a brand name), you don't spend more than you earn and you even have money left to save.

I saved a certain amount, and I wasn't tempted, like many others, to invest in all kinds of get-rich-quick schemes that generate profits only for those who pressure you to invest in them. I was focused on one thing and one thing only: real estate.

And then I was offered a partnership with a man from another city who loved "all kinds of bargains."

"Bargains" meant business opportunities with "potential." Some people are experts at that type of thing.

The idea is like this: You buy the roof rights of an existing building, build a few apartments on it and rent them out. The price of a roof is much less than an apartment, and construction costs are also cheap when you hire the contractor yourself. This way, you get an apartment at a price you can afford (with a mortgage, of course). And if you're really successful, you divide the apartment into two or three units and enjoy the rental income. I'm pretty sure you know what I'm talking about.

So, the two of us bought a roof together. I put in the money I'd saved up and took out a mortgage, he did the same, and then we began to build.

One day he told me that he didn't have any liquid assets right then, so it would be best if I paid for the construction, and he'd pay me back later from the rent.

Money was tight for me too, so I tried to get out of it, but he said, "Okay, no problem. Let's wait a few years." I got the unspoken threat: "If you don't pay, I'll get you." I took out loans and paid cash for the construction myself.

A few days after the construction was completed, he said, "Great. I've got some people lined up to rent at a good price."

I was happy to hear that.

Little did I know...

The tenants moved into the apartments, and all was well.

Or so I thought.

At the end of the month, I went to collect the rent from them.

"What's with the money?" I asked.

"We paid a year in advance."

"Who did you pay?"

"The landlord," they said. "Who are you?"

"I'm also the landlord here."

"Well, we didn't know that."

I met with my partner and got straight to the point. "How could you do something like that?"

"What's the problem?"

"You owe me for the building costs."

"Huh? What makes you think I owe you?"

I felt dizzy. "Because I paid for it, that's why."

"Wrong. I paid at the beginning too. Besides, this whole business was my idea, and I have no idea how much you paid. I suspect you made some kind of a deal with the contractor to my detriment."

I looked him straight in the eye. "Is that what you want to be? A cheat?"

"Me? A cheat?" he said. "You're the cheat! Just you wait and see. I'll do some investigating and expose everything."

It dawned on me that I was dealing with a con artist. No two ways about it.

"I'm taking you to *beis din*," I told him.

"Then I have nothing more to say to you," he replied.

That's another technique con artists use, to act offended when it's to their advantage.

The *beis din* summoned him, but he didn't appear. He didn't show up for the second summons, either.

At the third summons, he appeared and said, "The plaintiff has to use a *beis din* of the defendant's choosing. I want to go somewhere else."

The *dayanim* told me, and I also knew for myself, that this was the halachah. I had no choice. I went to a *beis din* of his choosing where I signed an arbitration agreement.

I want to tell you something about those few words: "I signed an arbitration agreement." I don't just want to say something, I want to shout it.

Be very, very cautious about signing an arbitration agreement. People don't know what it means. Your signature on this document puts your property, your money, and your future in the hands of one or three people.

By law, once you sign an arbitration agreement, the arbiter can decide whatever he wants without needing to explain how he reached his decision.

An arbitrator can write in the arbitration record that the agreement you signed will have legal validity *forever.* In other words, should another disagreement arise regarding the same property or even a different piece of property or even things only slightly related to this arbitration, the arbiter can still decide whatever he wants without having to explain how he reached his decision.

It turns out that arbitration is one of the most dangerous things in the world. Once you've signed, your life belongs to someone else, and if that person isn't worthy of his position, you're in trouble. And if that person is a con artist, you just might lose your whole world with that one signature.

An arbiter is almost omnipotent. He has no superior to whom you can go to question his ruling, and if you get permission from the *beis din* to take the case to civil court, most of the time, you'll lose, because the courts will tell you, "You signed? Stand by your word." You would have to prove in an irrefutable way that you were deceived or that someone got bribed. Such things are very difficult, almost impossible, to prove.

When you lose at arbitration, it's not just that you lose a few shekels. Sometimes you lose the whole property you went to arbitration for. Worse, now you have a new partner: the arbiter. Once you signed the paper he gave you, he can extend his authority until…someone stops him. And that's exactly the problem: There's no one to stop a destructive arbitrator. There just isn't.

But I didn't know that. So I signed.

Fifteen minutes after the hearing began, I realized that my world had been destroyed.

The arbitrator listened to my former partner, who slandered me and claimed that I was trying to take over the property, that I was a fraudster and a thief and had padded the costs, and that he had paid much more than he was supposed to.

"That's a lie. I didn't pad any costs."

"Let him talk!" the arbiter thundered.

I remained silent, but inside I was burning up as I waited for my turn to answer.

But then the arbiter said, "Both of you step outside."

We left the room. I assumed he needed to have a private conversation or something. I felt like I was about to explode because I was bursting to tell my side of the story.

When we were called back into the room, the arbiter declared, "Well then, the defendant will enjoy the fruits of the lease for five years. After that, he will have the right to purchase the property at cost price from the plaintiff. Thank you."

I thought I was going to pass out. "You haven't heard my claims!" I protested.

"I heard," said the arbiter. "You claimed that you didn't inflate the costs, but I was convinced that you had."

"But I had more claims."

"So why didn't you make them?"

"Because you told me to remain silent."

"I told you to remain silent when he was talking, but you didn't say anything after that."

I stood up and shouted, "I'm not going to listen to you! You're nothing but a cheat!"

"Then I have nothing to say to you," he said. "Get out of here."

I got up and left.

I started to cry. I couldn't believe what they'd just done to me. I ran after the arbiter and said, "You robbed me! How can you do something like that?"

He made no reply at first, but then he said, "Do I have to call the police?" and off he drove in his luxury car.

Anyone who knows me will tell you I'm a regular guy, but at that moment, I was as close to going crazy as I've ever been.

Suddenly I knew what it felt like to be stomped on by a monster. I'd just been trampled into the ground. Robbed of my money and my property.

I started calling friends. Some of them said, "Hello? Why in the world did you sign an arbitration agreement? That guy is known as an unfair arbiter. He must have gotten money from the other side."

Others responded: "Listen, if that's how he ruled, then that's probably the way it's supposed to be according to halachah.

Everyone who loses in *beis din* is unhappy about it. You shouldn't go around talking about, though. It doesn't look good."

I arrived home despondent. I had no idea what to do.

For two weeks, I brooded in silence. That was my first mistake.

People who experience trauma cope in one of three ways: fight, flight, or freeze. I couldn't fight because I had no power. I couldn't flee because I had nowhere to go. That left me with the last option. I withdrew into a kind of deep depression. I didn't even tell my wife about it. I was afraid she'd break down, too, and the whole house would collapse.

In the end, my wife got me to tell her what had happened

"We both know that the truth is on your side," she said, "and that you were robbed. Let's fight back."

"What can we do?" I said.

"We'll just go tell everyone we know. That's the best weapon I know of, the truth."

We started telling family, neighbors, and friends. That's when we realized how badly we'd been burned.

"Once you signed," they told us, "it was all over. He's a very powerful person. He'll fight you to the end."

There were some who weren't willing to give up. They appealed to a highly respected *beis din* where they persuaded the judges of the wrong done to me, and we were issued a permit to go to civil court.

But by the time this was accomplished, forty-five days had passed. We used a regular lawyer and got this laconic answer from the court: "We see no special reason to disqualify the arbiter. You agreed to take him when you signed the agreement, and his reasoning seems judicious. In all probability, he made the necessary inquiries. The fact that you've remained silent for forty-five days works to your detriment."

The arbitration was not invalidated. The ruling remained final. I'd lost the property. And let's not forget, I still had to pay the mortgage each month.

I never would have thought I'd reach such a low place mentally and physically.

It can't be that our world looks like this, I told myself. *I can't live in a world where the evildoer laughs and the righteous person cries.*

Terrible thoughts came to me, thoughts of deep despair and hopelessness.

Once again, my righteous wife got me out of the mental box I was in and forced me to get up and go to *kollel*. But inside, I was hurt and still licking my wounds at how I'd been trampled and still wondering how they could do something like that to me.

One day I saw a young boy pushing an elderly man in a wheelchair. They were going up a hill, and I saw that he was having trouble pushing the wheelchair.

I walked over to them and said, "Can I can help you?"

"Thanks," the boy said. "Another minute and I would have given up."

"Where are you headed?" I asked.

"We're on our way to my cousin's wedding. The man in the wheelchair is our uncle, and I offered to bring him."

The hall was some distance away, but no one else was around to help them get there. I began pushing the wheelchair. After about fifteen minutes of strenuous walking—it's not easy to push a wheelchair, especially with an adult in it and especially uphill—we arrived at the hall.

"Thank you, sir," the man in the wheelchair said. "He will continue on from here."

"One who begins a mitzvah should finish it," I said. "I'll bring you up to the hall."

We took the elevator to the hall and discovered that the chuppah was taking place that very moment.

I offered to take the grandfather upstairs. It was very hard, and I needed to recruit two other people to help me. We were barely able to get the wheelchair up the stairs, but we did, and so the man in the wheelchair was able to participate in his relative's wedding.

As I was bringing him closer to the chuppah, a voice announced, "We invite—" and here they said a very familiar name "—for the last blessing."

The name was that of the arbiter who'd destroyed my life.

He didn't see me, but I saw him all too well.

I watched his every move. He stepped up onto the chuppah platform, and then suddenly—I spotted another familiar figure.

One of the fathers was none other than my partner, the one who'd robbed me.

Trembling, I asked the man in the wheelchair, "Whose wedding is this?"

He told me the names of both sides. The groom's father was my thieving partner.

"What's his connection to the arbiter?" I asked him, trying to sound calm and feeling anything but. "He's being honored with *berachah achrita*, the final blessing, no less."

"Well, the arbiter's mother's maiden name is—" It was the same last name as that of my partner. "The groom's father is his uncle, his mother's brother."

I will never in my life forget that moment.

I waited for the man to finish the blessing and for everyone to say mazel tov, and then I stepped in front of the arbiter and said, "Mazel tov. The final blessing, huh?"

The man's face changed colors and not due to the honor he'd been given. "What are you doing here?" he asked.

"It doesn't matter what I'm doing here," I said. "The question is, what are *you* doing here. But that's not really the question. Here's the grateful uncle repaying the person who helped him rob people. Give me the microphone so I can tell everyone how special your uncle is and how appreciative."

I ran to the microphone, and he ran after me and stopped me. "Don't ruin the wedding," he said quietly, and then added in an undertone, "We'll work it out."

I hadn't planned on ruining the couple's joyous moment. I'd just wanted to scare him.

I went home and told my wife what doing that *chesed* brought me, and we both cried softly and knew that our suffering had come to an end.

The next day the partner called me. "We need to talk," he said.

We met within half an hour.

"Tell me what you want," he said.

"Within the next twenty-four hours, I want you to transfer to me the rents you have received to date and to continue transferring to me all the rental income you get in the next year until I get back everything I've invested in the properties. Likewise, I want you to take care of getting a new *psak din* from your own *personal* arbiter. And make sure it's an honest *psak din*. I sincerely hope that I won't even have to argue."

"And that's it? Is that what you're asking for?"

"Yes," I said. "I know that if you were me, you'd ask for full ownership of the property in perpetuity. I also know that your fear is not only about you, but your nephew, the rogue arbiter. He's the one pressuring you to come to terms with me. So tell him that I'm an honest man, not a swindler like you. I just want what's due me. Nothing more."

Within two hours, I received a new "ruling" along with a very substantial check: all that year's rental money from the two apartments, plus repayment of everything I'd spent on construction. It added up to enough for me to invest in a new project.

Sometime later, I learned that I was not the only one he had swindled. My partner had played similar tricks on many people, always using the method of being the one who's sued so that he gets to choose the *beis din*. We're talking about people who would have no way of knowing the familial relationship between them. Naturally, I wanted to let people know about it, but I felt it was too big for me to take on. I contacted a Rav who said that if I felt it was more than I could handle, I wasn't obligated to.

I know there'll be a lot of people who'll criticize me for this, and to them, I say, "Don't judge a person until you stand in his shoes. You don't know what I went through and what it did to me. Even the thought of it causes me real anguish in the deepest parts of my soul."

The only thing I can do is to write this story to you and warn people about arbitration. I don't want to generalize. Most institutions and *batei din* operate according to halachah, especially when they are composed of three *dayanim* who must decide together. What I'm trying to warn people about is to be very careful about signing an arbitration agreement and to let them know that they have the right to restrict the arbiter's power to one specific case and one specific time. And I want to emphasize that people should check carefully to make sure the arbiter has no vested interest in the case and is not a relative of the plaintiff or defendant.

We need to realize that the temptation to go to arbitration is great because sometimes millions are at stake, but even a few tens of thousands of shekels are enough to make the arbitrator act unfairly.

And let's not forget the reward for doing a kindness.

You have no idea how hard it was for me to push that wheelchair. There was a part of me that wanted to pretend I hadn't seen the boy struggling with it. I didn't really have the time or the energy right then. But in the end, my decision to help both the boy and the man in the wheelchair is what brought me to the right place at the right time. That small kindness I did turned into a huge kindness for my family and me.

What Does a Mikvah Purify?

A family on their way back to authentic Judaism wants to establish a mikvah in their settlement.

They run into a firm refusal from the council head.

They ask anyone who might possibly help to lend a hand, but no one's willing. Until they reach the commander of the air force base, who presents everyone with a "fact."

A heartwarming story. A surprising story. And most of all, a purifying story.

When I heard you tell your wonderful story about the mikvah in Bhamdoun, Lebanon, it immediately brought to mind a similarly amazing story I knew firsthand, and in fact, the two stories are connected.

I live near Gedera, and my story is not about the mikvah in Bhamdoun but about two mikvahs here in Israel that were harder to build than the one in Bhamdoun.

It all began in the Aseret settlement, which is a ten-minute drive from Gedera. Aseret was founded by religious immigrants from Hungary, but their children did not follow in their footsteps. By the way, out of dozens of settlements in this region and its neighboring region, Nachal Sorek, only two remained Orthodox in every way: Yesodot and Beit Chilkiya. If you ever decide to investigate the reasons for this, you'll have a great story of its own.

Back to Aseret.

We received a request from two local families who told us there was no mikvah in the settlement, and they were interested in having one built. They also gave us a tip: the founders of Aseret had built a mikvah, but over the years it had closed, and the Bezeq company had taken over the building. But it was clearly registered as a mikvah. All they wanted was help and the funds to renovate and restore the structure to its intended purpose.

We contacted the Taharat Habayit organization of Rav Mutzafi, *shlita*. They contacted Bezeq and asked them to vacate the building. Bezeq agreed, and members of Taharat Habayit began to renovate, which is something they do every day of the year in dozens of places.

Only here they were in for an unpleasant surprise.

The head of the local council decided that he did not agree to let a mikvah be built in his community. He summoned the Border Police, no less, to stop the work and board up the building. Don't ask me what connection the Border Police has with a mikvah in Aseret, but that's what happened. "I respect religion, but this isn't a religious place, and I absolutely do not agree that there will be a mikvah here," is what he told Rav Mutzafi.

The council's head, Weiss, was a member of the Likud

Central Committee. Members of Taharat Habayit began to exert pressure on him by sending Likud members to talk him into giving in, but it was like talking to a wall. Even Sarah Netanyahu tried talking to him but couldn't get him to change his mind. The Taharat Habayit people managed to convene a committee in the Interior Ministry, and when you say "committee," that's usually the end of the story. And not for the better.

The mikvah renovations stopped.

Now I'd like to tell you another story. This one took place a few years earlier. But as you'll see later on, the stories eventually merge.

Taharat Habayit put in a request to build a mikvah at the Ovda Air Force Base.

Rav Mutzafi himself went there. In his honor, they set up a large conference table at which all the commanders sat waiting for the base commander.

As soon as the base commander entered the room, everyone stood up in his honor. He threw his keys on the table and said, "What's on the agenda?" And then he saw Rav Mutzafi. "What is the Rav doing here?"

"I came to build a mikvah here," Rav Mutzafi said.

"Too bad you made such a long trip for nothing," the base commander told him. "Sorry, but there'll be no mikvah here on my base."

"Why not?" asked Rav Mutzafi.

"Let me put it like this," the base commander said. "What would happen if I brought two fighter jets to Ponevezh Yeshivah? Would you agree to put them in the yard?"

"First of all, bring them," Rav Mutzafi replied. "Besides, Ponevezh doesn't need planes, but here, a mikvah is needed.

We didn't come here out of the blue. There are lots of families here, and there is a demand."

"Not a problem. For anyone who wants a mikvah, I'll arrange a ride to Bnei Brak. They can take a dip there."

"It doesn't work that way," Rav Mutzafi replied. "People won't travel for a mikvah. They want one here. What's your problem with approving it? You don't have to pay for it."

"I've got nothing to do with religion. I eat on Yom Kippur, and my wife is even worse than I am."

"There is no worse," Rav Mutzafi told him.

Rav Mutzafi sat down and explained the importance of the matter, until the base commander softened up and said, "Well, put in a request. I'll pass it on to the higherups."

The Taharat Habayit people prepared permits and then ensured that the permits would reach the then Minister of Defense, Ehud Barak. Nine months later, they began to build.

Two weeks later, Rav Mutzafi received a call from the base commander. He thought he'd be in hot water—and not that of a mikvah. But he was wrong.

"The workers haven't shown up for the past two days," the base commander said. "Why?"

Rav Mutzafi wondered why he was asking. He'd been so opposed, yet now…

He made some phone calls and got back to the commander. "A few of the Sudanese and Eritrean workers, and some Arabs, too, are having trouble getting past the checkpoints."

"Send them to me," the commander said. "I'll give them permits, so they don't delay the mikvah."

After a while, the base commander called up Rav Mutzafi and said, "I want you to open the mikvah on July 10."

"Okay," replied Rav Mutzafi, not daring to ask why the sudden interest. "What do you want me to buy you in honor of the opening?"

"I'm traveling to France," the commander said. "I won't wear a *kippah*, but tzitzit under the uniform, yes. For my wife, Shabbat candlesticks."

"Your wife, the one who's worse than you?"

"Yes, the one who's worse than me," the commander said.

July 10 arrived, and there was a beautiful ceremony to mark the opening of the mikvah as well as a party for all the soldiers. Someone jokingly said to the commander, "Say a *dvar Torah*."

The base commander spoke. "I've seen all kinds of Jews. There are Sephardim and Ashkenazim, and even chassidim with the strange name of Merachem Rivkah—" (he meant Rachmistrivka) "—but they all have one thing in common no matter where they are in the world, and that's mikvah. It's a sign that it's something truly pure."

At the end of the celebration, the commander asked Rav Mutzafi to "arrange a meeting for me with an international rabbi before I go to France."

Rav Mutzafi brought him to Rabbi Chaim Kanievsky, *shlita*, introducing him as the commander of an air force base who helped build a mikvah.

"Blessing and success," Rav Chaim said.

"I didn't come to get a blessing. I came to bless the Rav."

"Why do I need you to bless me?"

"I was told that I was coming to a great international rabbi. I thought I would come to a fancy place, a palace. But when I came, I saw such a simple place. I want to bless you that there be many more like you among the Jewish people."

"Amen," Rav Chaim answered him.

Then Rav Chaim said, "I bless you that you'll have healthy children."

As soon as he said that, the tough-as-nails base commander started to cry. No one knew why, and no one dared ask.

Erev Rosh Hashanah, Rav Mutzafi received a phone call from the base commander.

"I have a story you've never heard," the base commander said. "You must have noticed that at first, I didn't agree to build a mikvah, but then I took to the idea. Now I'll tell you what was behind it. My wife and I have been married fifteen years. Two years after our marriage, we had a son.

"As soon as he was born, they found out that he had a rare disease caused by a genetic incompatibility between us. Don't you chareidim do a test at Dor Yesharim? Well, that's just it. We didn't. Our son passed away when he was only a few years old.

"Over the years, several children were born to us, and they all passed away one after the other. You have no idea of the grief and pain we went through. What does a *chiloni* like me do? I threw myself into my work here in the army. As you can see, I made my way up the ladder to become a base commander.

"Once I was piloting a plane that was on its way to attack when they suddenly told me, 'You have a phone call.'

"The prime minister was on the line.

"'I'm sorry to have to tell you this,' the prime minister said, 'but another son of yours has died.' That was the third one to die. 'You are released. Get off the plane and go home.'

"'Mr. Prime Minister,' I told him, 'I will complete my mission and then go home.'

"A week later, you arrived at the base. I was so bitter that I said to myself there would be no mikvah here. Your organization contacted various influential people, and the Ministry of Defense gave the go-ahead. I said to myself, 'Fine. I'll make sure it never happens.'

"But a week later, my wife and I were contacted by a prestigious American research institute. We'd pulled strings to get accepted into their research program, and now they were calling to say they'd gotten the funding and we were in.

"The doctor who spoke with me said, 'I'm Jewish like you, and I'm Orthodox. You don't have to, and it has nothing to do with the study either, but I highly recommend that you keep the laws of family purity.'

"It was so close to the story with the mikvah that I couldn't dismiss it as coincidence.

"'Right now,' I told him, 'people want to build a mikvah on my base.'

"'Wonderful,' he said to me. 'That's perfect for you.'

"Remember when I called you and asked why the construction was being delayed? Now you know why.

"They did the research studies, and we returned to Israel, and just then, the dedication of the mikvah took place. Then you brought me to your rabbi. I actually had wanted to ask him for a blessing, but I was too proud to do so.

"Then, all of a sudden, he gave me a blessing that my children will be healthy. It packed such a powerful punch because none of the people there knew anything about our troubles. Even you were hearing it for the first time. 'How did he know?' I asked myself. 'It must be *ruach hakodesh*.'

"A week later, my wife and I traveled to France with your tzitzit and candlesticks. Suddenly I got a call from one of the secretaries who transferred me to a doctor who told me excitedly, 'We want to let you know that your problem is a simple one that can be solved with one pill. Too bad you didn't come to us sooner.'

"'What have we got to lose?' I said to my wife. 'Let's give it a try. What could happen?'

"Well, something did happen. Genetic tests showed that this child doesn't suffer from the same disorder our other children died of. Your rabbi's blessing was fulfilled in full."

"Can I ask you to participate in an event dedicated to strengthening family purity?" Rav Mutzafi asked him immediately.

"Why not?" the commander said. "When I'm back in Israel, I'll attend."

When the commander returned to Israel, Rav Mutzafi mentioned to him the stalled mikveh project in Aseret.

"Why aren't things moving forward?" the commander asked.

"The head of the council is against it."

"I know him," said the commander. "We're close. I'll drive over there and tell him my story."

He kept his word. He sat with the head of the council for two hours, telling him his story. The man called Rav Mutzafi right away. "I've been persuaded. I'm giving my approval for building the mikvah."

End of story, right? That's what I thought too. But there's more.

In a conversation between Rav Mutzafi and the council head after he'd approved the mikveh, Rav Mutzafi asked him, "Tell me something. Between you and me, what was the real reason for your opposition to the mikvah?"

His reply will leave you and your readers open-mouthed. Because this just might be a story that's even more interesting and more important than the first two.

"As a child, I attended a religious school," the council head said, "and one day, I was thrown out of school along with two of my friends. There was no special reason. All they said was that our families weren't all that religious, so we didn't fit the school.

"I could have been the chief rabbi," the council head said. "But someone got up on the wrong side of the bed that day and decided I wasn't a good fit for religion. He threw me out of school and out of religion straight into troubled waters. The anger I felt at that time has grown stronger over the years."

The mikvah at Aseret is being built right now. But it's important for everyone to know the three stories behind it.

If you ask me, the first person who should enter that mikveh is the person who cut off three Jewish children from their heritage without first consulting with a spiritual leader just because it seemed okay to him.

I'm going to end by bringing the Mishnah in *Yoma*, Chapter 8, Mishnah 9, which ties in these two amazing stories:

"Rabbi Akiva said, 'Fortunate are you, Yisrael! Before Whom do you purify yourselves, and Who purifies you? Your Father in Heaven. Just as a mikvah purifies the impure, so does Hashem purify Yisrael.'"

A Leadership Drive

A teacher in a quiet moshav decides to take his students on a trip.

In the absence of a bus, he loads everyone into his car.

He's going to pay for this mistake with his driver's license (and rightly so).

Is there anything that can mitigate his punishment?

The fascinating story I want to tell you happened to me personally. My main purpose in sharing it is to convey the message that simple faith can help every single Jew in every type of situation.

I used to teach afternoons in a yeshivah for younger boys. There were about fifteen boys in my class.

It was several days before the *bein hazmanim* break in Nissan. Only those who teach can testify along with me how difficult it is to teach during this time, and to what extent the boys are no longer able to concentrate during *seder.*

Some teachers lose kids at such times because they don't understand what their students are going through. They respond by becoming tougher with them, sometimes even speaking harshly to them, and within a short time, they lose the close relationship they've painstakingly built up over the previous months.

I had the *siyatta diShemaya* to recognize the situation for what it was, and I was careful not to go head-to-head with my students but instead to organize all kinds of trips and activities to give them some form of release. Mostly, I wanted to make sure they stayed within the yeshivah framework. Sure their attention spans were less, and they found it hard to concentrate. But they were still on track, still trying to learn well, and I rewarded them for it.

They'd gotten to know me and knew I wouldn't let them down.

One afternoon, I found the boys tired and desperate for a break. I caught on right away that even learning for half an hour was beyond them—even if I promised them a trip to the Alps.

"Let's learn for five minutes, and then we're off," I announced. "We'll go to one of the nearby communities and chill out with a good game."

Since I'm used to making snap decisions, I didn't give much thought to the logistics.

I forgot to mention one thing: I was a fairly new driver at this time, and I had a small car worth a paltry four thousand shekels.

Obviously, I couldn't fit everyone in the car. To take some of them and return for the rest was out of the question because one never knows if anyone would be there when I returned. It's more than a little irresponsible to leave boys alone for even five minutes.

When the boys noticed my indecision, they said they wanted to try to squeeze all of them into my car.

"It's only a five-minute drive!" they pleaded. "One road, and we're there."

Before I could respond to their wild idea, I found myself driving the car, which seats five, with nine boys squished inside plus another one in the trunk.

I'm sure everyone reading this will be highly critical of me, and rightly so. I don't have much to say in my defense other than the fact that the moshav is a quiet, out-of-the-way place with no vehicular traffic. Picture a field with me putting everyone in a horse-drawn wagon and galloping ahead. Doesn't that make it sound more reasonable?

I guess not.

I was wrong. I admit it. But what can you do?

Anyway, I stepped on the gas and drove slowly and carefully.

Murphy's Law entered the picture when suddenly I spotted a car behind me, signaling me to pull over. I ignored it and kept on driving.

The car bypassed me and signaled me to stop.

It was not a police car, so I ignored it and continued driving. All of a sudden, I was asked by the driver over a loudspeaker to stop immediately. That's when it dawned on me that the car was—are you ready for this?—an unmarked police car.

I got out of the car, knowing that there went my driver's license. *It was nice being a driver for a few months*, I thought.

The policeman knew exactly why he had stopped me. "Open the door," he said.

I did, and a couple of boys fell out.

"Get out, get out," he ordered. And just like in the stories, he started counting: "One, two, three, four, five, six, seven, eight, nine!"

Then the boy in the trunk peeked out.

"Ten?! Are you crazy?" he shouted—or, to be more accurate, bellowed. "Just what do you think you're doing?"

Face flushed red with anger, he grabbed my driver's license and the car registration, took the keys, then called for backup and a tow truck.

I could hardly breathe. I felt my knees begin to buckle.

"You're right!" I cried out. "I made a very big mistake! I don't know why I did it. I just weighed one thing against the other and decided it was better for me to cram them into the car than leave some behind without supervision. It's also a really short ride, less than five minutes. I know I wasn't thinking straight, and it certainly doesn't demonstrate much intelligence, but that's what went through my mind."

I saw he was about to let me have it, and I realized that no amount of explaining would help, so all I said was, "You're right! Take the license, take the registration, take the keys, take everything! I probably don't deserve to be a driver. Everything is from Above, and I deserve it."

The policeman was stunned. Evidently, his anger had come from a place deep inside him, not solely from his duty as a policeman.

"Do you really believe that everything is from Above?" he asked. "From Above, you had to break the law and put these boys at risk?"

"No," I replied. "I admit that I broke the law and in a serious way. I really don't think Hashem wanted me to break the law, but neither do I think that I endangered the boys in this short drive in this quiet place. And I think you know that, too. But you know that police patrol cars don't pass this way, so think about why you suddenly happened to be here. I'm sure you'll agree with me that it wasn't a coincidence. And so, I can only conclude that I deserve this from Above. Things don't just happen. My license was taken from me from Above so I wouldn't be able to drive."

At that point, the boys came over to us and said to the policeman, "Officer, please go easy on him. He's the greatest rebbi and the best guy in the world. He really cares about us and does everything he can for us, and he never makes a big deal out of it if we make mistakes."

One of them—a bit brashly, I must admit—said, "Sir, it's not him, it's us. He's a serious person. He would never have done such a stupid thing in his life. He just caught it from us. I'm telling the truth!"

The policeman couldn't help but smile.

Then another boy spoke up. "Sir, try to understand him. Our rebbi always exaggerates. He gives everything all he's got. Without making calculations. Even now, he didn't calculate how many boys there were, he just put us in."

It was as bad as it sounds, and the policeman looked at me and made a gesture with his hand that said, "He said it, not me."

I thought I was going to have a heart attack, but I saw that it softened him up.

One boy after the other came over to put in a few good words about me: "Officer, he could have told on me to the principal a thousand times and had me kicked out. Give him a chance. I'll be responsible for making sure he doesn't take more than seven or eight kids."

Stuff like that.

One sensitive boy came over and just started crying. "Officer, please take pity on him. He doesn't deserve to suffer."

He made me start crying, too, that sweet kid.

The policeman didn't know what to do, and then he asked, "Tell me something. Do you believe what you said before about this being from Above, or did you say that just to get me off your back?"

"No, I do believe that everything is from Above. Even if it is to my detriment, it's for my benefit."

"If so," he said, "if you truly believe that everything is truly from Above, and I see that you understand the seriousness of what you did, I'll give you a summons to a trial in one month. There, from Above, the judge will decide what to do with you."

He whipped out his walkie-talkie, canceled the tow truck, and then handed me back my license, registration, and keys. He asked five boys to get into his car, five of them got in mine, and that's how we went back.

I didn't know how to thank him.

"May it be Hashem's will," I told him, "that the judgment of the court here below will satisfy any punishment that I would have received from the court Above."

But I also wanted to atone for the desecration of Hashem's Name that I caused, so I asked him to come to our class to give a talk on road safety. It was important for me to admit to the students that I hadn't behaved properly. When all is said and done, I do serve as a role model.

The policeman agreed. After a short conversation, I

discovered that he was none other than the regional police chief, not just an ordinary patrolman.

The next day he arrived with another policeman. The students' behavior was exemplary. They paid attention to the talk and participated exceptionally well.

The policeman came out thrilled. "What a class! What students! What a privilege to teach them. I've never spoken in front of yeshivah students before. What an upbringing they get. I've never seen anything like it in my life."

I was happy a *kiddush Hashem* came out of it, but the story was not over yet.

The policeman was so impressed that he wanted to surprise the students by letting them see a demonstration of police tracking dogs, as a tribute to the Israeli police force.

What an extraordinary experience my students enjoyed that day.

The students were respectful and well-mannered. The policeman was even more impressed than he had been from his previous encounter with them.

He thanked the principal for inviting him and even told the principal that he was fortunate to have a teacher like me.

I felt like I had atoned in some measure for my terrible wrongdoing.

He didn't cancel the court summons, though. It wasn't in his power to do so, and I knew that. But we became friends. He saw more sides to me, not just the part of me that pulled such a ridiculous stunt that sorry day.

One day, I got a call from the policeman. I was excited to

hear from him to begin with and doubly excited when I heard why he'd called.

In just a few more days, he told me, a ceremony to affix mezuzos at Yosef's tomb in Shechem was scheduled to take place, with higher-ups from the police, army, and transportation ministries in attendance. As is well known, you can't get to Yosef's tomb without a police escort. Since he would be driving there in a patrol car with a team of policemen, he was offering me the opportunity of going with them so I could pray at the tomb.

I thought I was dreaming. I'd never been there, and here Hashem was sending me a chauffeured ride with free security protection.

I was supposed to go with him late at night. During the day, he called and asked if I wanted them to come with the patrol car to pick me up at home.

I tactfully refused. I didn't want the neighbors to think I was being arrested. I asked him to wait for me at the city's exit, which I'd get to on my own.

My workday ended, and I got a call from the policeman. I headed for the city's exit.

Senior police officers surrounded our patrol car. They asked the policeman (who by now was a close friend) who I was.

He answered them that I was a rabbi in the city, giving me a wink in the rearview mirror.

We arrived at Yosef's tomb. Military and police personnel were already there. The mezuzah installation ceremony began.

The policeman signaled to me that I should say Kabbalas Ol Malchus Shamayim. I raised my voice in prayer. There was electricity in the air. I saw the policeman's eyes glistening with tears.

"I didn't know you were a chazzan, too," he told me on the way back.

"I don't understand how I had the merit to have you bring me here, to the tomb of Yosef Hatzaddik."

"Well, Yosef Hatzaddik was imprisoned for an extra two years because of the extra words he said: *z'chartani* and *hizkartani*—*remember me* and *mention me.* When I caught you, you also said words that seemingly didn't need to be said: 'Everything is from Above.' With those words of faith, you made a *tikkun* for the words of Yosef Hatzaddik."

I smiled. "I didn't know you were a maven about reincarnation."

Since then, our friendship has grown stronger. I've invited him to handle security at events I organize, and we've gotten into a lot of conversations about Judaism. He grew more and more interested and even began to set aside times to learn Torah.

But wait! I still haven't told you what happened at the trial.

I appeared in court a month after the incident. My friend the policeman gave me a few tips on how to act there, but the truth is that I mainly trusted in Hashem and tried to repeat constantly, "*Ein Od Milvado.*"

The judge was an Arab. He read the indictment, was shocked at what had taken place, and began to question me.

I told the judge that first of all, I'd made a mistake, but I'd done it in all innocence because I was afraid to leave a bunch of rambunctious boys alone while I drove only some of them. I added that I also volunteer to rescue at-risk youth all over the country.

The prosecutor who filed the complaint sat there, adding to the proceedings. He voiced the opinion that my license should be revoked for as long as possible because the passengers were children.

And then...

The policeman entered the hall.

He stated his name and rank and said that he was the one who had issued the ticket. He told the judge that although he had not been summoned to court—because there was no dispute regarding the facts of the case—he decided to come on his own.

He told the judge he had nothing to say about the gravity of the offense and that it was indeed a serious offense. He described the scene at it was: a quiet moshav without vehicular traffic, I was driving carefully, and that apart from the serious violation of the law, there was no real danger to the boys.

He said he hadn't come to minimize the seriousness of the offense, but only to tell the judge a story.

Apparently, everyone loves stories. Even judges.

He told about the boys who came and pleaded with him, who said I was an "awesome rebbi" (everyone there laughed) and that I'd probably caught their foolishness... And that in the same way I overlook their nonsense, could he please overlook the nonsense of their awesome rebbi?

"Look, your honor," the policeman said, "my job is to make sure there are no bad drivers on the road. This man might have been a bad driver, but as a teacher, he seems to me to be exemplary. I wish everyone were like him,

"Still, we don't want bad drivers on the road, even if they are excellent teachers, so I'll tell you something, your honor. This man admitted his mistake immediately! He said, 'I don't deserve a license. And it must be Heaven's will that my license be taken away.' A statement like that is only made by someone who takes responsibility. I've also been observing him these past few months. He has clearly internalized what happened, so I can state with full confidence that he is no longer a bad driver. That's all I have to say," the officer said, ending his testimony.

It was quiet. The judge turned to the prosecutor and said to him, "So, what do we have here? A good teacher, a driver who was a bad driver and then became a good driver. What do you say?"

The prosecutor, still under the impression of the story, said, "I was definitely impressed by the character witness testimony, and I will rescind the request for a three-year cancellation of his license. One month's suspension plus a two-hundred-shekel fine will be enough."

The judge agreed. The verdict was signed.

I couldn't believe my ears. I left the courtroom overjoyed, thanking Hashem for all the kindness He had shown me and for giving me the wisdom, insight, and intelligence to atone for my actions by making a *kiddush Hashem* instead of enduring punishment through human hands, and I knew it was all in the merit of *emunah*.

When my friend the policeman he heard the court ruling, he smiled and said, "One who believes isn't afraid. Hashem is with you. No doubt about it, you got off easy. Even in my rosiest dreams, I didn't think it would end like this!"

"A person who trusts in Hashem will be surrounded by kindness," I told him.

I learned an important thing: First of all, make sure to abide by all the rules of road safety, and if a police officer stops you, it's because he was sent by Hashem to guard and protect us, or so we could be messengers to make a *kiddush Hashem*.

In the case of this policeman, he was real. He didn't do his job because he enjoyed seeing me lose money or because he wanted to see me taken off the road.

His sincerity brought the message home to me at that moment. I felt remorse for what I'd done.

It made me realize that when we're angry with our children or students, if we feel real pain, they'll be receptive to us.

A Match Made in Heaven

A young son-in-law enters the family. It's a perfect match all around until…

Until an unanticipated conflict crops up that creates a gap between them as vast as the distance between heaven and earth.

And when someone tries to bridge the gap, the whole country hears about it.

I can't wait to tell you my story. Though it makes me look a bit foolish, my wife and I learned a lot from it.

Everything is completely true except for the few minor changes I've made to disguise the identities of the major players.

I got married a few years ago. My wife is amazing. She's full of life and very supportive. We're a perfect match in so many ways, including the similarity between our families. It was, as they say, a match made in Heaven. And soon you'll see that this expression will take on another meaning...

Life decided to teach us that even if we thought that

everything was flowing smoothly, well, that's just it, we thought it was. Life is about coping with issues that come up. I know that what we had to cope with may seem like nothing to some people but bear with me, and you'll find out that under certain circumstances, it can be a huge problem.

My wife's family had a tradition that every summer, they flew abroad to visit the elderly grandmother. It meant a lot to the grandmother, and her feelings were hurt if anyone was missing. In hushed tones, the family would hope that the absent party wouldn't lose out on their share of the inheritance.

I'm talking about an entire family, father and mother, children—most of whom were already married—and grandchildren. The group totals some thirty people.

Then what's the problem? Who wouldn't want to take a trip like that to such a generous grandmother?

So it's like this. The way to get to Savta's home abroad is through a mode of transportation called a plane.

The only catch is that the new son-in-law who's just entered the family, who happens to be yours truly, suffers from fear of flying.

A few words about this fear.

This is a fear so strong that I can't even picture a situation in which I would enter a vehicle that will be lifting its wheels from the ground and hovering in the air.

As far as I'm concerned, it's not even a question; just like most people would never think of jumping out of a plane even with a parachute. I've always known this is something I can't do, and I accepted it.

The truth is that when my wife and I were dating, she did mention something about the annual family trips abroad to visit the grandmother. I joked that I had a fear of flying, and we left it at that. I have no idea why neither of us thought it was an important issue. Maybe because nothing seemed like an issue then. She thought I would understand the situation and get used to traveling, and I, having no direct experience with "the whole family is flying abroad," innocently thought that it wouldn't be such a big deal if we skipped the visit. The absolute truth? I didn't think about it even once. It just wasn't an issue.

We were married at the beginning of the winter, a time when the visit wasn't a topic of conversation, and, like I told you, the early days of our marriage as newlyweds were wonderful, the kind every couple wishes for themselves. Pesach arrived and soon after Lag BaOmer, and then everyone started talking about the trip—where they'd stay, for how many days, and so on.

The whole family was caught up in it. There was no other topic of conversation, just where to go and what to do and how to get there and if everyone would take different flights or be on the same plane or—

Plane? Uh-oh.

I watched as my wife got all involved in the planning full steam ahead to the extent that, because it was so clear that we were going along with everyone else, it didn't even come up for discussion between the two of us. After all, the grandmother was paying, so that was taken care of. There was nothing left to discuss, and all the questions revolved around what to buy for the trip and who to sit next to on the plane.

Again, the plane.

I realized I had to make myself clear before it was too late.

At the first opportunity, I tried to explain to my wife about the terrible fear that grips me every time I think about flying. I told her I just couldn't see myself doing it.

Her initial response was to dismiss it. Of course. "Once you're on the plane and feel how steady it is in the sky," she told me, "you'll sleep through the whole flight."

I made it clear to her that, unfortunately, this was a very serious issue, and there was absolutely no way I was doing it, at least not in my current lifetime.

"Wait a minute," she said to me. "If you're afraid of flying, how do you plan on us going to visit Savta?"

It didn't occur to her that there might be the glimmer of a possibility that I was trying to tell her that….

I didn't know what to say, so I just kept quiet.

"Answer me," she said.

"I'm trying to tell you that…we can't go visit her."

I don't wish on anyone to have to face what I faced after dropping a bombshell like that on my wife. And it really was a bombshell. I still didn't understand fully, but from her shocked expression, I began to realize that there was a serious problem here.

"You can't do this to me," she said.

I had nothing to say to her.

And that's where the whole mess started. A campaign of phone calls to the whole family about how Yossi isn't willing to travel, and he insists, and so on.

They couldn't believe what they were hearing. Everyone told her, "Put him on the phone. It'll be okay." Every brother-in-law tried to tell me, "Don't worry about it. Sit next to me, take a pill, I had the same thing, it's only five hours." After they came to realize it was a little more complex than that, they started coming over to see me in person.

Each of them sat down to have a serious talk with me. They told me how important it was for the whole family and certainly for my wife, who was an integral part of the visit each year, and how hard it would be for her if we didn't go.

I had to explain to each and every one that I was eager to be part of the family trip but that it was so difficult for me that it was virtually impossible.

The only people who can understand this fear of flying are those who suffer from it themselves. It's not something you can control. You're just scared to death of hanging there in the sky, suspended between heaven and earth! And despite my strong desire to make my wife happy and not spoil her plans, I just couldn't do it.

You don't want to know how awful those days were. I hope your readers will understand what my wife stood to lose out on and how seriously disappointed she was.

At a certain point, my wife came to realize that I just couldn't do it. I think her father must have talked to her about it. The pressure level went down, but with it, so did the mood. The minute she grasped that we were not going to be traveling with everyone else on the annual trip, she got depressed, and there's nothing worse for a husband than to see his wife sad. I was ready to jump into a fiery furnace if only not to see her like that. But for me, taking a flight was a lot more frightening than any fiery furnace.

I suggested that she go without me. She refused to even consider the idea, even though we were a young couple who didn't have children yet. "I always dreamed that when I got married, I'd bring my husband on this trip to visit my grandmother. Do you really think I want to go there alone and be the object of everyone's pity? Not happening."

I was forced into a difficult situation. All the members of the family were busy getting ready for the trip, planning the activities, and remembering the fun had by all on previous trips, while my wife sat on the sidelines, devastated that this time she was not going to be part of the trip.

I couldn't wait for the visit to be over and for everyone to return home safely, so that we could go back to normal, with happy communication like always. The closer we got to the trip, the more emotional everything became. The shopping sprees to get ready for the trip brought another rush of excitement. And it goes without saying that the whole family left for the airport together from her parents' house. We were there to say goodbye.

We returned home from Ben Gurion, and then things got hard. Very hard. My wife cried a lot. She felt that everyone was off having a good time while she was stuck at home because of some kind of fear that came from who knows where and why did it even have to exist. I tried to cheer her up, but that only made things worse.

In the morning, the feelings burst out again. She had to go to work while everyone else was probably unpacking their bags at the grandmother's, and then later, we were eating a plain old regular dinner while everyone was enjoying a meal fit for a king overseas.

It was hard. Her distress filled the sharp silence of our home. I didn't know how much more of it I could take. I felt like the bad guy, a cruel monster who was keeping his wife from doing what she'd looked forward to from the moment last year's trip was over.

And then the visit ended. Again we were there for them, this time to welcome them home while politely asking them how it went. Then the stories started. Stories about all the special experiences, the hilarious incidents during the flight. Then one of the brothers-in-law came over to me, patted me on the shoulder, and asked in a loud voice, "So, how was it back home? Did you have a good time? Tell us all about it," and everyone burst out laughing.

I tried to go with the flow, so I bantered back, saying we'd wanted to go to an amusement park, but when we heard they had planes there, we decided it wasn't such a good idea. For some strange reason, the joke fell flat, leaving me feeling worse than ever.

It took weeks for everyone to return to normal. Aside from occasional brief mentions of the visit, the topic dropped out of sight.

So, the trip was no longer being talked about, but deep down, I knew the situation couldn't continue like this. I could find a way to deal with my own feelings, but what about my wife? Would she have to sit on the sidelines each year watching the production? Would she have to endure a situation so difficult for her year after year?

That's when I made a decision. What happened this year would not be repeated next year. I would have to do for me the unthinkable: jump into the water. I didn't know how I'd do it, but I knew I was going to get on a plane. I was afraid to make any promises to my wife in case I backed out. It was my own personal secret.

The *chagim* went by, then Chanukah, too, and I knew that if I wanted to be ready for the end of the year, my first trial by fire was definitely not going to be in front of an audience. I didn't need any more humiliation in that department. An idea came to me. We'd try it on a domestic flight in Israel, just to gradually break the fear. It was winter, when tourism isn't at a peak and prices are low, so the idea was perfect.

I decided to surprise my wife. She deserved it, didn't she? I first called her place of work to check which days she could be absent from work. I got dates for the end of the following week, from Tuesday to Thursday night. My heart began pounding. As far as I was concerned, I was walking straight into a fiery furnace. I'd be suspended between heaven and earth!

My hands were shaking when I called and ordered tickets. I told myself, if you have second thoughts, the worst that can happen is that you lose the money. Dozens of times, I decided not to go ahead with it, that I just couldn't. But deep inside, I knew that I had no choice but to try.

The day before the flight, I took out our suitcases and opened them in the living room. When my wife came home from work, she was surprised. What was going on? I laid the tickets on the table. Her amazement was total.

"You're going on a plane? I don't believe it!"

I explained to her that it was very important to me that we travel with everyone else that summer, and I wanted to try to gradually get rid of the fear. Her joy had no limits. The happiness of knowing that the big dream was not buried forever, but that there was a chance, made her the happiest woman on earth. We packed up, and my heart fluttered. Now there was no turning back. I wasn't going to cancel now. Not a chance.

That night, I didn't close my eyes for a second. In the morning in shul, when I greeted friends, they puzzled over the heartfelt "shalom" I gave them. For me, it was sort of like saying goodbye for the last time.

My wife's parents drove us to the airport. I was on the receiving end of congratulations and compliments like, "Good for you! You're a real hero!"

We reached the airport. We waited in the security check line nervously. My throat was dry, my eyes darted in all directions, and I drank from a bottle of water constantly. The security guards saw a person sweating, looking around in all directions, obviously under terrible pressure.

"Is everything okay?" the security guard asked me.

I answered yes, but my body language was screaming the exact opposite. Based on their scrutiny of our belongings, I realized that my tense facial expression conveyed that I must be smuggling heavy weapons.

We made our way to boarding. I was hoping against hope that something would happen and the plane wouldn't arrive. Can't it happen that a plane doesn't show up? That the pilot is sick? Flu, a cold? What? Pilots aren't human beings?

Everything was against me. Meaning, everything went smoothly. The plane arrived. The pilot was in good health, and I found myself living through my worst nightmare.

I boarded the plane.

We sat down. I was wiping the sweat from my forehead constantly. I could hardly breathe. I asked the flight attendant if she could take down the oxygen kit from above. The flight attendant looked at me like I had fallen from the moon, or worse, from the plane. My wife burst out laughing and told me that the oxygen kit is only released if the plane is in an emergency situation before a crash or a forced landing.

It was not a good idea to say that. Not now. Not to me. Not at all.

My wife tried to smooth it over by explaining to me that, statistically, there was a greater chance of being injured in a car accident than from an aircraft malfunction, and that there were almost no aircraft accidents. “Almost” is not something you say to someone who’s scared.

An authoritative announcement to buckle seat belts came over a speaker. I’d been buckled up from the second I sat down. The wheels started rolling on the black asphalt. The plane’s speed became frightening.

And then, after a few hundred yards, I felt like my legs were no longer supported, and I realized that we were in the air. My heart pounded wildly. I couldn’t breathe. The plane straightened out and started a smooth flight. People around me were yawning and closing their eyes to sleep, but I knew I had to stay awake so that in case anything happened, I could let the pilot know.

As the minutes went by, the tension lessened slightly. Very slightly. The feeling of stability on the plane made me realize that disaster doesn’t strike every flight. There may be some flights where it doesn’t.

The landing was actually less traumatic, maybe because my fear is fear of flying and landing marks the end of a flight. Why didn’t I think of that?

From there, things got really good. I felt like the first person to land on the moon. Phone calls from the whole family and friends.

"I did it," I told everyone, and my wife was proud and happy.

We spent two days there on a great vacation, better than anything I remembered. My wife appreciated what I'd done and realized that now she'd be able to travel with her family.

I pushed off thinking about the flight back. It was as if we would be staying there forever, until the day we died. My denial lasted two days, until the moment we returned to the airport.

When we arrived at the aging airport, my worries came back with a vengeance and grew more intense as we boarded an old plane.

The pilot turned off the lights and wished us all a pleasant rest. And again, the flight was smooth. There were no unusual events.

In the middle of the flight, I felt the need to use the restroom. I got up my courage and went to the back of the plane. One of the crew members came out of the cabin at the back of the plane, and I asked him where the door to the restroom was. He pointed. If he said so, he probably knew what he was talking about. I walked confidently to the back of the plane, where I saw a kind of electric handle with an arrow on it pointing down. I said to myself, "Good thing there's an arrow. Otherwise I wouldn't know which direction to push the handle."

I started to push the handle down.

Nothing prepared me for what happened next.

All at once, the entire rear area of the plane was illuminated with blinding light. A deafening siren began to wail. Before I even could guess at what was going on, the steward, who had been so nice and polite, jumped on me from behind and frantically pulled me back and pushed me to the floor.

"What do you think you're doing?" he screamed.

He threw me onto the last seat of the plane, sat down next to me so that I couldn't move, and told me, "Don't you dare move from here even for a moment."

As if that wasn't enough, the pilot himself appeared, demanding to know what was going on.

I began to hear passengers shouting.

"What happened?"

"Is everything okay?"

"Is this an emergency?"

Then I heard the flight attendant quickly explain to the pilot, "This fellow tried to open the plane door. I stopped him at the last second."

I couldn't understand why he was making up a story like that.

According to procedures, in exceptional situations such as this, the captain must get authorization from the control tower for every action he takes. He contacted them fast and reported that there was a passenger who, for some as yet unknown reason, tried to open the plan's emergency exit. He was instructed to return the handle to its original position and to question me thoroughly.

The situation was bizarre. I was sitting there in the last seat, surrounded by stern-looking staff members, who didn't know whether it was a terrorist attack or a suicide attempt, trying to get information from me. I saw my wife standing behind them crying, and all around were panic-stricken passengers trying to figure out if they'd be getting home safely that day.

They bombarded me with questions, and I said, "All I wanted was to use the restroom. You pointed to this door."

All the flight attendant's courtesy and diplomacy were gone. "Are you blind?" he said. "Are you pretending not to know what an airplane is?"

"He really doesn't know what a plane is," a voice said.

It was my wife.

"He has a fear of flying. This is the first time he's flying, and he did it for me."

They were not convinced that fast. They looked at me and then at her and asked if this was really the first time I was flying.

"No," I told them. "This is the second time. The first time was two days ago on the way there! But this is really the first time I went to the restroom on a plane."

This broke the tension somewhat. But they weren't buying my story just yet. They looked at each other and continued to bombard me with questions. They asked me for details of my identity and checked them against my ID until finally, they were convinced that I was a normal passenger without any malicious plans.

They told me to return to my seat. Now I was supposed to walk all the way back to my seat with dozens of pairs of eyes staring at me from every direction.

When I got to my seat, the passenger who'd sat next to me at the beginning of the flight got scared. He stood up, mumbled something I couldn't catch, and made his way down the aisle toward the back of the plane. I guess he wasn't taking any chances.

From then on, every minute or so, I saw a passenger lift his head to check up on me, to make sure I wasn't trying to break a window, lift the shutter, drill a hole in the plane's floor, or who knows what.

Actually, only then did I realize that of all the passengers, I was the most relaxed. It was an incredible awareness. I, the one who's afraid of flying, was sitting there on a plane with everyone around me more scared than I was.

My wife was upset and embarrassed. I was scared she would become afraid of flying or something...

I tried to explain to her that the way the handle was marked was really misleading, but go tell that to someone who's flown countless times.

We landed.

I was afraid that the Border Police would be waiting there for me at the exit, but no, no such thing. We went to the baggage carousel. We stood on one side, and all the other passengers preferred, for safety reasons, to wait on the other side. They also called their relatives to say that they'd been saved from certain death and that the person trying to open the plane door was still right there in front of them.

We took the suitcase, entered a taxi, and headed home. I asked my wife in the strongest terms possible to please not tell anyone about the incident. I didn't have to spell out why.

On Friday night, we went to her parents' house. Naturally, the entire family gathered to hear about our trip and, naturally, to hear how the flight was. My wife tried very hard to say how much fun it was and how much we enjoyed it and that everything was fine.

Then later, during the meal, her older brother walked in and said, "Did you hear the news? On the flight to Sde Dov, some weirdo passenger created a panic on the plane when he tried to open the door. What kind of nutcase would do something like that?"

"What?" everyone asked. "Really? What was he trying to do?"

"I don't know," the brother replied. "They say he thought

it was the bathroom door. What an idiot! He couldn't tell the difference?"

Our breaths caught. It had made the news?! The blood drained from my face. I was shocked. I tried to change the topic of conversation, but they didn't need extra-sharp vision to see the shock and confusion on both my wife's face and mine.

"Wait a minute," the brother said. "Did this happen on your flight? Why didn't you tell them about it?"

A moment of silence. And another moment. No one said anything, but apparently, everyone added one plus one, and it suddenly dawned on everyone there that the weirdo passenger, the nutcase, and idiot was sitting right there in front of them. Who knew if he wasn't about to open some window right then and there.

And as if by a hidden switch, everyone started laughing.

They laughed like I'd never seen them laugh before. I tried to say, "It wasn't funny. I thought it was the door to the restroom!" Which made them laugh even harder.

Then help came from heaven. It was my wife, who'd been there and who understood my distress.

"What do you all say?" she said. "How about inviting Savta to Israel this year? You see how hard it was for Yossi, yet he still tried so hard to overcome the impossible, just for me. Maybe it's time to pay him back? How about if we try to think out of the box and come up with a family plan to convince Savta to come?"

After a few moments of silence, her father got up and declared, "I'm all for it! Yossi deserves it." Then, as if planned, every single person there said, "This year we'll go up north and rent a big place with a pool."

Sure enough, the unbelievable took place. Right after Pesach, the family closed with a villa owner in a quiet settlement in the north. I was overjoyed. We were involved in every stage of planning and preparation. We traveled in the family car, one of several vehicles making the trip. It was a lot of fun, with plenty of activities such as hikes and outdoor attractions. At the end of the trip everyone said they couldn't remember such a challenging and fun trip. We did the same thing the next summer, spending the time here in Israel.

I knew how to appreciate their sacrifice.

First of all, I appreciate my wife's sacrifice, for if you didn't understand the difficulty at the beginning of the story, I'm sure you do now. Despite her great disappointment, she accepted my anxiety and agreed to pay the price, which, you have to admit, was not cheap.

But her family also deserves the warmest words. It's obvious to me that they made a huge concession for a close-knit family member who suffers from anxiety they don't really understand so that he and his wife would feel good. And they didn't even complain. On the contrary, they said it was the best thing in the world for them. That's truly a sacrifice that comes from good *middos*, done in the most beautiful way imaginable.

I intend to try to pay them back—to try to travel during the next summer vacation to visit Savta abroad. I hope I succeed. One thing I know for sure. If I do get up from my seat, I'm sure there'll be a volunteer to accompany me no matter where I go, just to make sure. You know what I mean. After all, statistics show that no one ever goes to open a plane door. Almost.

In conclusion, if anyone has any questions about the veracity of this story, they can check the date January 29, 2016 / 19 Shevat, 5776, and find my story under the headline "Israeli Passenger Confuses Airplane Emergency Exit for Bathroom In-flight."

Well, I am the passenger, and you can certainly trust me on this. Just don't come asking why I don't open any doors for you.

A Slap Across the Face

A multimillionaire philanthropist comes to visit an educational institution in danger of closure.

As is customary, the institution puts on its best face and prepares an elegant reception ceremony.

There's only one thing they didn't take into account: that the philanthropist will be given an unimaginable surprise during his visit.

Will the institution survive the blow?

I've been following your stories for many years, and I've noticed that in almost every story, there's a moment when you touch on some deep inner point that reveals hidden feelings and makes readers cry whether they want to or not.

I've been keeping a story like that inside me for many years.

For decades, I've worked in a well-known treatment facility somewhere in Israel. I don't want to give any details, and you'll see why later. The patients are autistic and disabled children of all ages, with numerous problems. Half are with us on an outpatient basis and are bused home every night, and the rest have conditions so severe that they sleep at the institution, which becomes their home, with their parents occasionally coming to visit.

Or not.

These children and teens are anxious to associate with normative society, but for some reason, that normative society distances itself from them and would rather put them away someplace, so they don't become a burden on it or disturb its smooth functioning. These are children who are not so communicative, and the task of raising them ranges from difficult to unbearable to even impossible.

Many of these children are virtually abandoned. No one is overly interested in their welfare. As far as society is concerned, "they're being taken care of," which makes the institution's managers and therapists sort of exclusive rulers over their lives. While there is oversight that is supposed to prevent disgraceful situations of neglect and abuse, most things depend on the goodwill of the institution's directors and direct caregivers. Take, for example, food, heat, and air conditioning. These are things that can't be overseen from a distance, and sometimes, whether out of reluctance to invest in a good heating system or even just out of laziness or carelessness, boys shiver from the freezing cold in the winter and come down with pneumonia and other complications. Because of their inability to communicate, the children can't complain, and if they protest in a different way, the staff, if they are unfeeling, may severely punish them, and no one will hear their cries for help.

I know I may be shocking many readers, and some will even turn the page so they don't have to hear or imagine what autistic children are going through, but I feel obligated to shout this to the heavens before I start my story.

The facility in which I worked was complex. Due to budgetary constraints, there was less manpower than needed, as well as a lack of funds for basic comforts. The staff, which was conscientious and devoted, did its job well, but had to cope with the tight budget management put at its disposal, and also with management that, though it did everything it could, wasn't the most professional.

Let me explain. As far as dealing with the authorities and obtaining funds to keep the facility going, the management did a good job. They did whatever they could, and the managers weren't granting themselves fat salaries at the expense of their charges. They were people with good intentions who didn't have an understanding of the essence of the institution they had established. They knew how to run it as far as the administration went but lacked the right approach and the knowledge of how to deal with the type of problems that needed to be tackled and resolved.

This caused constant tension between the staff, who fought for benefits for their charges, and the management, who invariably rejected ideas and requests for efficiency and improvement, whether due to budget deficits or lack of understanding.

They were very tough, the managers. We always felt that they would be better suited running a for-profit company than an institution that works with souls. On the other hand, that's what there was, and there weren't many people standing in line waiting to open such a facility.

Among the staff was a righteous, gentle woman named Shifra. She literally gave her heart and soul for the sake of the children. She never argued about her salary, and often paid out of pocket for basic items like heaters whose purchase the management hadn't approved. We knew her work and valued her, but management valued her less. They saw her as a provocative figure in opposition to the management, but we knew the word "opposition" wasn't part of her vocabulary. She was genuinely worried about the children, and her "battles" were fought very naively, without creating power struggles and without any backup.

The result was that management did everything it could to make her quit. They didn't give her a single promotion and tried to block her in every way.

We saw it and kept quiet. After all, we were worried about our own jobs, and most people don't want to fight city hall, even if not doing so requires one's conscience to make compromises.

One day, the management of the facility announced that a big philanthropist would be visiting and that they hoped he would make a substantial donation.

The staff was instructed to decorate the classrooms and all other rooms, as well as to prepare the children to impress the philanthropist and his entourage. The truth is, it was next to impossible. I want to point out again that these children were noncommunicative, with severe autism and retardation. The kind no other educational system could absorb.

But we did the best we could, especially as far as making the place more attractive and dressing the children in clean clothes and making them look presentable. Someone also brought music and tried to rehearse the children in a performance of something like "Ring Around the Rosie." More than that could not be expected, especially when no funds were given to prepare the event.

The big day arrived. The walls of the facility had been painted, at least in the areas that the philanthropist and his entourage were supposed to pass by, and we all waited together with our charges for their arrival.

They made a tour of the institution, and then they reached the dining room and passed by the children, who didn't really respond and barely moved to the sound of the poor-quality music.

There were a few speeches. The kids didn't even know what was going on. A few of them started to make noise, and the staff member who was in charge quickly whisked them away.

Then, without any advance planning, the philanthropist decided to go closer to the children.

He went over to each one and said, "What's your name?" Not a single one of the kids answered him. Some also reacted nervously, because these were children who had difficulty coping with changes to their routine and with unfamiliar faces, and here they were being challenged by both.

Then the philanthropist approached a fourteen-year-old boy whom Shifra, the staff member I told you about, was responsible for. The philanthropist moved closer to the boy and said, "What's your name?"

And suddenly it happened.

The boy slapped the man across the face. Hard. Every single person there heard it. Everyone held his breath.

Everyone but one person: the boy himself.

Because now that he was worked up, he pulled the expensive

gold-rimmed glasses off the face of the stunned philanthropist and snapped them in two.

After the shocked silence, pandemonium broke out.

The director ran over to the philanthropist and pulled him away from the boy while shouting to Shifra, "Get him out of here!" Then he led away the battered philanthropist while someone picked up the two halves of the broken glasses.

I don't think this ever happened in any institution that wanted to raise money from someone. It was obvious to all of us that no donation would be forthcoming that day. The question was, what would happen to the institution and especially to Shifra.

Where was Shifra in all this? She was busy calming the boy, quietly singing him a song, as if he hadn't just slapped a multi-millionaire across the face, and as if he hadn't just broken that same millionaire's expensive glasses.

The philanthropist looked at her and at the boy and didn't say a word. To anyone watching, it looked like a provocation on Shifra's part. Only we knew that it was just Shifra being Shifra. She was just focused on her responsibility. But to tell the truth, we also thought it was a bit much. With all due respect to the child, he'd just done something very problematic, and there was a hurt philanthropist there, so maybe the right thing to do would have been to remove the child and calm him down somewhere else.

Anyway, that was the end of that event. The director escorted the injured philanthropist (double meaning intended) to his car. The entourage disappeared into their vehicles but not before sending hostile looks at the director, and the caravan left the place with screeching tires that sounded particularly loud.

Now the director ran back to the dining room. Shifra was still there, still fully focused on her child.

"You're still here? Pack up your stuff and get out of here!" he roared.

Shifra looked at him, stunned. She was really and truly shocked. We watched as tears formed in her eyes only to spill over in a growing stream.

I'll never forget her look at that moment. It was one of total surprise. And the tears were tears of overwhelming grief.

She whispered to the boy, "Come, I'll take you to the room," and began to walk with him. The director took a few threatening steps toward them but stopped suddenly. What could he do? It was too late.

"You ruined half a year's worth of work!" he shouted after her. "This philanthropist is so stingy that to get him here, I had to invest a fortune. Now everything is down the drain, all because of you and your foolishness!"

Shifra just kept walking and crying, and we all knew that those were her last steps in the facility. We felt a terrible sadness overcome us, and an unbearable heaviness settle over us. We saw her take her briefcase and walk out in silence, and we knew that at that very moment, the heart of this facility was getting up and leaving. Or, more accurately, had been shamelessly banished.

Two days passed, days with an undercurrent of tension. The truth is, we were all worried about what would happen because from what management had declared in recent days, it was understood that this philanthropist represented the facility's last chance of survival. We were all waiting for notification of downsizing or closure. We realized that our hopes of things improving were quickly fading and that not only would the current situation not continue but that things would become even worse.

But on the third day, right in the middle of the day, a car drove up to the facility, and who should get out if not that very same philanthropist.

He walked in accompanied by one assistant, without any entourage, and asked to speak to the staff.

We were all called. It took some time to gather our charges and hand them over to the supervision of three staff members and some interns. The whole team quickly gathered.

They seated him at the head of the table. He said, "I don't know what you know about me, but I'm not known as a big donor. I donate, but to a very limited number of institutions, and not one of them is...of this type. My contributions go more toward scholarships for outstanding students and the like.

"Someone took advantage of connections with someone who had pull, and I had no choice but to come here. I knew I was coming because I owed someone, and I knew that nothing would come out of it because I don't like being manipulated.

"I took a look around the place, and it's not nice to say, but it didn't do anything to me. It was no different than what I had imagined, and rooms and decorations never do it for me.

"When I saw the children, I felt a little pity, because every human being feels sorry for unfortunate children, but it still did not change my approach, that aside from a small one-time donation which I would have given anyway, I wasn't going to invest anything here.

"But then I went over to that boy. I don't know what I was trying to see in his eyes, maybe a spark of connection or understanding. I'd once found the whole subject of autism interesting until other things began to interest me.

"And then...

"I got slapped in the face, hard, down to the bone.

"When I was a kid, I'd gotten a few slaps, but since then, no one's lifted a hand to me. And I'd never gotten a slap like that in my entire life.

"As if that wasn't enough, the boy broke my glasses. It didn't interfere with my vision, because they were for seeing close-up. I can see things at a distance just fine.

"And see I did.

"I saw everyone's panic and the director's anger, which I could understand. That boy had just ruined all his hopes and dreams. Even though I knew they were false hopes and dreams, he didn't know that.

"What amazed me in all this mess was his teacher's reaction. She had absolutely zero interest in the calculations people around her were making. She was focused on the boy, calming him down and taking care of him. She wasn't angry in the least.

"Only two people in the dining room had a completely different understanding of the whole situation. The first was that teacher. And the second was me.

"I've been a businessman for decades, and whenever there's innovation, I'm the first to spot it.

"The slap shook me up, and not because of the physical pain. That was secondary. This slap woke me up and made me understand, understand that this child has parents who deal with it three hundred and sixty-five days a year, thirty days a month, seven days a week, and twenty-four hours a day. They will give this child everything, but all they'll get from him is slaps, and they will understand, or not, that this is their destiny.

"Suddenly, I realized that an institution like this shares the slaps and the coping, with the parents. The staff is on the receiving end daily of slaps like the one I got, and it handles them the way it handles them. How did I know? Because I saw that woman, the teacher, and I knew.

"On the drive home, I was churning. My assistants realized I was going through something and offered to call up the director and tell him off, and all sorts of things that they thought would calm me down, but I firmly forbade them from taking any action, whether good or bad. I announced that anyone who tried to protect my honor would no longer be in my employ.

"Yes, I was very upset. When I got home, I touched my sore cheek and felt it was my soul hurting. And then I remembered that teacher who cared so much for the boy, exactly at those moments, and suddenly I began to cry bitterly, letting out the anguish that had been bottled up inside me on the ride home. And I knew, as I cried, that I was going to transform that place into a palace, a place that could give those kids everything they needed, which meant first of all more staff, more and better treatment rooms, clothing and beds, a new kitchen and the best food there is.

"I've come here with a check for several million shekels, and I've even assigned someone to be in charge of spending the money in a way that will transform the institution into what I dreamed of for it. I have only one condition."

He paused, and we all held our breath.

"I want the director to appoint that teacher to oversee the changes. I don't want her to be a financial manager. I don't want her to be running to the banks or flattering donors. I just want her to tell my people where the money should be spent. I trust her implicitly. She knows what these kids need, how much staff to add, and what needs fixing.

"I know I'm setting myself up for trouble because if she didn't take into account the slap I got, she surely won't take into account my money. She'll think about the kids. But I'll give her a free hand. Naturally, only with management's agreement. By the way, where is she?"

An awkward silence filled the room. No one knew where she was, but we all knew why she wasn't there.

No one dared to speak.

"She's taking the day off," the director said. "Can someone please ask her to come here now?"

I volunteered.

I ran to the office and called her. "Shifra, sit down," I said. "You've got to get here."

"But I was fired. You know that, don't you?"

"Yes, I know it, but don't ask what's going on here. The philanthropist came back and he wants to donate, but only if you'll be the one deciding what to do with the money. Please come."

I heard her gasp. "But it will take me half an hour. The bus here—"

"Take a taxi," I interrupted. "The institution will pay for it. Just come."

"Okay," she said. "I'm coming."

I quietly returned to the staff room and said she was taking a taxi to get here.

A discussion began, with each staff member making suggestions, whether about how many staff members per child or about the renovations and innovations.

"You can all relax," the philanthropist said. "The check in my hand will cover everything you want several times over. But I very much ask that you agree to my request to entrust the decisions to that teacher."

"Her name is Shifra."

"Shifra," he said. "What an appropriate name. Shifra was

one of the Hebrew midwives who cared for the helpless children. Very appropriate," he repeated. "I'm sure she'll listen to you."

* * *

She came. The director of the institution went out to greet her, apologized profusely and asked her not to tell anyone what had happened.

It was unnecessary. Anyone who knew Shifra knew that such a thing would not have occurred to her.

She just appeared. The philanthropist sang her praises, then suddenly he stopped when tears filled his eyes as was happening to the staff members as well. I'd never seen anything like it in my life.

When he finished, she said, "I agree on the condition that the director of the institution agrees."

The director of the institution said, "Of course. Certainly. With pleasure."

Then Shifra said to the philanthropist, "I apologize to you for that slap. Tuvia didn't know what he was doing, and every time I get a slap, I feel it's like a caress from Above. The slap you got was worth a few good slaps, so you can really be satisfied."

Everyone laughed, releasing the tension and relaxing the atmosphere. The meeting ended.

Many years have passed since then. From being a second-rate or even third-rate institution, this institution became one of the top such places in the country, and even gained international renown as a leader in the field. To the philanthropist and his family, the place became their baby. Never before had they taken such a personal interest in a project or poured so much money into it.

Shifra is still in her position, and as long as she holds her position, I know those funds will go to the right places for the benefit of the helpless children.

And if you ever thought a slap was a bad thing, maybe you'll change your mind.

Sometimes we need a slap to wake us up.

The Last Wish of David the Gabbai

A shul without a minyan is not a happy sight—especially for the gabbai.

But that's exactly the situation faced by David the Gabbai in the Pardes Katz neighborhood.

Somehow, he connects with a young avreich who restores life to the synagogue—and to him as well.

What neither of them knows is that the story of David the Gabbai's death will be even more intriguing than the story of his life.

Chaim Walder, I've been sitting on the story I'm about to tell you for a good number of years. It might have gone to the grave with me if I hadn't gotten into a situation—and there is no such thing as coincidence—where I needed to daven Minchah when I was in one of the office towers in Bnei Brak.

To save time, I decided to drive to Itzkowitz. I pulled out of the underground parking lot and drove down Rechov

Abuhatzeira. That would lead me straight to Sokolov and from there to Itzkowitz. But when I ran into a traffic jam on Rechov Baruch Hirsch, I realized I wouldn't make it in time. I decided to look around the neighborhood for a shul. I was driving down Abuhatzeira when I saw a sign that said, "Beit Knesset Kol Yaakov." I parked the car and made it just in time for Shemoneh Esrei. Then I stayed for Maariv.

Between Minchah and Maariv, memories of this particular shul washed over me. Until only a few years earlier it had been little more than a shed tucked away next to a flower shop that later became the Taboon bakery, for those who remember, and it was now surrounded by skyscrapers which, in the urban development of the area, had sprung up like mushrooms after rain.

This synagogue was only active on Shabbos, and right then was empty of congregants. The reason was simple enough. It was an Ashkenazi synagogue in the Pardes Katz neighborhood. *Pardes* means "orchard," but there were no orchards anymore, and Katz was the only Ashkenazi name in the neighborhood.

In case you don't know, the Pardes Katz neighborhood was founded by Hungarian immigrants and consisted of orchards and dairies. Holocaust survivors joined the original settlers and operated dairies. For Minchah and Maariv, they'd tie up their horse and wagon outside the shul to daven.

Over the years, the orchards and cowsheds became garages and residential buildings. Immigrants poured into the neighborhood from Morocco, Libya, and Tunisia, and everyone knows how badly they were discriminated against and weren't helped to integrate. Pardes Katz was transformed from a rural settlement into a distressed neighborhood, the Hungarian immigrants moved out, and the synagogue was eventually left with elderly men and one gabbai named David Weiss, who is the hero of our story.

For years, the synagogue was deserted, without a minyan except on Shabbos. Still, Reb David Weiss made a point of coming every day and "looking for a minyan" even on weekdays. It was as sad as it sounds. The synagogue fell through the cracks of its aging walls.

One day, a young *avreich* arrived at the synagogue. Later, I'll tell you his name and you'll discover that you know him well. He met Reb David Weiss, who was the person davening there that day, and what do you think he said?

"Would you agree to let me give a *shiur* here every day?"

Reb David Weiss looked at him like he was out of his mind. "As best as I can remember," he told him, "giving a *shiur* includes having an audience, and no matter where I look—east, west, north, or south—I don't see any audience here."

"Don't worry about it, Reb Yid," the enthusiastic *avreich* told him. "I just need your *beit knesset*. I'll take care of the participants—me and the Toda'ah organization I work for. You'll get a regular minyan for Minchah and Maariv here, *b'ezras Hashem*."

Reb David Weiss hadn't made such a good deal since he'd sold his barn to a developer. He agreed on the spot.

The *avreich* didn't waste any time. Posters plastered the neighborhood announcing the new Toda'ah *daf yomi* class at the Kol Yaakov Synagogue to be followed by Minchah-Maariv.

A week later, at the first class, Reb David Weiss was surprised to see a minyan of workmen walk into the shul, some of them still in their work clothes, and some with machine oil stains. They sat listening to the *shiur* and then davened Minchah-Maariv.

In between, the *avreich* spoke with Reb David, who turned out to be a very tight-lipped person for a Hungarian. He was a Holocaust survivor and apparently had been through some tough situations that he preferred to keep to himself. All he told the *avreich* was that he had two children who hadn't remained religious. Reb David was very close to them, but his heart ached over the fact that they hadn't followed in his footsteps. "I just hope there will be someone to say Kaddish for me," he said to the *avreich*.

The *shiur* drew more and more people to the place, turning Kol Yaakov into a shul with a *nusach* that varied. According to what? According to the *baal tefillah*.

If he was Sephardi (and he usually was Sephardi), it was *nusach Sephardi*. If he was Yemenite, it was Yemenite. If the *baal tefillah* was Ashkenazi, the davening was Ashkenazi. The hands were the hands of mechanics and drivers and builders and laborers, but the voice was the voice of "Kol Yaakov."

One day, Reb David Weiss told the young *avreich* that he was planning to move.

He lived in a one-story house across from what today is the Dudaim Hall. The place no longer suited elderly people like him and his wife. He told the *avreich*, "Reb Gershon, I'm moving to the city, and I place my trust in you that the *beit knesset* will continue with the *shiurim* and everything."

Reb David Weiss moved to Rechov Sokolov, corner of Hashelosha in Bnei Brak, and the *beit knesset* continued on without him.

Reb Gershon, the *avreich*, retained his connection with Reb David and suggested that he drive to the daily *shiur.*

"I have to help my wife," Reb David used to say.

One day, Reb David Weiss called Reb Gershon and said to him, "Come to my house. My wife died. I need you to help me."

Reb Gershon arranged the funeral and also a daily minyan for the week of mourning. He got to know the two children. One worked in the aerospace industry, and the other operated a tow truck. The sons, who had already heard about Reb Gershon, felt comfortable with him, and during the shivah told him they were worried about their elderly father, who was already having trouble living on his own.

"Until now, at least he was busy caring for our mother. Now we're worried that he'll be left alone, and, especially at night, who will look after him?"

Reb Gershon had an idea. As well as giving *shiurim*, he held the position of *rosh mesivta* at a nearby yeshivah.

"I have an idea," he told them. "We have a boy learning in our yeshivah who lives in Rishon Lezion and finds it hard to return home every evening. I suggest that he live with your father. He'll watch over him and help him in exchange for being able to sleep there."

The sons were pleased with this arrangement. They were very relieved that someone would sleep in the house with their father and take care of him, and at least relieve his loneliness.

Two years passed, during which Reb David traveled daily with Reb Gershon to the daily *shiur* and Minchah-Maariv. Shacharis and Shabbos, he davened at Beit Yehudah on Rechov Rav Shach, under the direction of Dayan Dov Domb, *shlita*.

Then elections for the Seventeenth Knesset rolled around. It was 2006, and Tommy Lapid had just left the Shinui party to form the "secular faction" in the "Chetz" (Arrow) party. This secular group was threatening the yeshivah world, and there was great concern that it would pick up where the anti-religious Shinui party had left off.

Rabbi Gershon asked Reb David if he was interested in voting for a religious party in the upcoming elections.

"Absolutely not," Reb David told him. "I don't believe in any party, and I'm not going to vote."

Two days later, Reb Gershon explained to him that "not voting" is actually voting for a party that hates religion, like Lapid's secular party. He also gave him an article to read that explained it, and that article convinced Reb David.

"If that's the way things are, then I'll vote for a religious party." Then he said, "Wait a minute," and did something inexplicable. He took his ID card out of the closet and placed it on a shelf outside the front door, under some leaflets.

"Look—I took out my ID card so that next week, you can remember where I put it."

It was Thursday, and election day was the following Tuesday. There was no rational reason for Reb David to put his ID card outside, especially not a week early.

But Reb Gershon said nothing.

Shabbos.

Reb Gershon ate the Shabbos morning *seudah* at his mother-in-law's house and then returned home to find two *bachurim* waiting for him outside.

"Are you Reb Gershon? Rav Domb is looking for you. He wants you to come to the shul immediately."

"What happened?" Reb Gershon asked.

The *bachurim* evaded the question. "Come with us. Rav Domb needs you urgently. Something happened in the shul."

"It's about Reb David Weiss, isn't it?"

They nodded.

"Did he— Did he pass away?"

"Yes. There's a police car there. They're looking for you."

Reb Gershon ran as fast as he could and arrived at the shul just as the police were about to remove the body of Reb David Weiss.

Apparently, Reb David had arrived at the synagogue as usual, but when everyone stood for Shemoneh Esrei, people noticed that he was still sitting with his tallis over his head. At first, they paid no attention. But when they saw that he didn't stand up for *birkas kohanim*, they lowered the tallis and discovered he was unconscious. They quickly called Hatzalah. When the responders arrived, they tried to resuscitate him but in vain. Reb David died wrapped in his tallis.

As is required by law, the police were called.

"Who knows this person?" was their first question.

Everyone knew the deceased and knew his name as well, but no one knew where he lived or to whom to turn. Only Rav Domb knew that Reb Gershon was in constant contact with the deceased, and so he sent two *bachurim* to go and bring him.

When Reb Gershon arrived, the police questioned him. He told them he knew the deceased and where he lived, but they needed more.

"We need his ID card," the policeman said. "We can't rely on your statements alone. Otherwise, we'll have to take him Abu Kabir."

Abu Kabir is a forensic institution that was notorious for routinely performing autopsies.

"How are we supposed to get his ID card?" someone asked.

"I'll bring it," Reb Gershon said.

Everyone looked at him in surprise.

"According to the law, no one is allowed to enter his home," the police informed him, "unless given permission by a household member, his wife, or children."

"His wife passed away, and his children don't live here," I said, "but I'll be able to bring you the ID card without entering his house."

You'll have to admit it sounded strange and even somewhat suspicious, but only one person in the world knew that the ID card was not in the house. And only now, two days after the strange action was taken, did he know why.

Reb Gershon went straight to Reb David's home, a three-minute walk away, walked over to the package of leaflets, and fished out from under them Reb David's ID card, which he had placed there in a most puzzling manner.

He returned with the ID card. The policemen relaxed and left, giving permission for the body to be left until *motza'ei Shabbos* with Rav Domb (whose standing as a *dayan* was like that of a judge).

Since Rav Domb had been guarding the body and dealing with the police, Reb Gershon offered to replace him so that he could go home for the *seudah*. Rabbi Domb agreed, and so Reb Gershon remained with the deceased with whom he had formed such a close relationship in recent years.

Two hours later, an old man arrived.

"I heard that Reb David passed away," he said. "I live here in the neighborhood a few blocks away and used to be his neighbor in Pardes Katz. I even davened with him at Kol Yaakov."

As they spoke, Reb Gershon discovered that not only did the elderly man know the deceased from Pardes Katz but that their friendship went all the way back to Hungary, where they had both lived on the same street.

Then the old man told him something about Reb David that no one else knew, and if not for him, most likely, no one would have ever known.

"Reb David's family had a flour factory, and when the Holocaust reached Hungary in 1944, catching everyone by surprise, he was able to hide dozens of sacks of flour and sustain hundreds of people, saving them from starvation for a long time.

"And then we were all transported to a concentration camp," the man said. "Reb David couldn't take along his sacks. On the train, he kept worrying, but it wasn't the same worry the rest of us had. He was pessimistic. It was clear to him that we were going to die. What worried him was that he wouldn't merit a Jewish burial. He told me, 'In the end, we'll all die. But we'll be a pile of ashes, or our bodies will be thrown out to the fields for the dogs to eat.'

"All the things we refused to believe for so many years, despite the eyewitness stories of survivors from areas already overrun by the Germans, blew up in our faces.

"When we arrived in Auschwitz, he somehow escaped being slaughtered. He risked his life daily and smuggled food to the hungry prisoners. Several times he was almost captured, and once he was caught red-handed and taken away by SS men. We all mourned him. Before they took him, he shouted out to us, 'Make sure they say Kaddish for me.' We knew that his prophecy of devastation had come true and that he wouldn't merit a Jewish burial.

"Two days later, he came back, half dead. In fact, he was much more than half dead. There were slim remnants of life in him. He'd gone through unspeakable abuse. His body survived, but his soul seemed to die there in Auschwitz.

"We immigrated to Israel, and against all odds, he raised a family, had children, and together we prayed there at the Kol Yaakov Synagogue. He became a very closed person. Everyone thought he'd always been that way, but not me. I knew what a happy person he'd been before the Nazis broke his body and almost killed him.

"When he was just starting out, he bought burial plots for himself and his wife in the Segula Cemetery in Petach Tikva. I remember how everyone laughed at him. What was the big rush to buy a burial plot at his age? But I knew that as far as he was concerned, it gave him a sense of security.

"People don't have their priorities straight. They cry about a deal that didn't go through or about not having a fancy car and don't understand the dreams we had in the Holocaust. Being buried like a Jew was a *dream* that not everyone dared dream and that most didn't merit to have. So when he bought those graves, he was fulfilling the dream.

"I eventually moved from Pardes Katz to live with my children, and he joined me a few years later. Now he dared to dream of another luxury: 'I don't need a big funeral,' he told me. 'But I hope that at least there'll be a minyan to say Kaddish for me.'

"And now he was privileged to die with a tallis on and not have his body dragged off to Abu Kabir. He's right here in the shul, and *b'ezras Hashem* on *motza'ei Shabbos* he'll have a funeral, and I believe there will be more than a minyan there."

Tears sprung to Reb Gershon's eyes. Only now did he understand how Hashem had led him to this abandoned shed between the flower shop and the bakery. Now he understood why there was an election and why Reb David had so strangely placed his ID card outside the house. All the pieces of the puzzle fell into place, and he knew he was going to arrange for this precious Jew the most distinguished funeral he could ever have dreamed of when he was alive.

As soon as Shabbos was over, Reb Gershon phoned one of Reb David's sons with trepidation.

"What's up?" the son asked.

"Your father didn't feel well on Shabbos."

"How is he now?"

"He's in shul."

"Why not at home?"

"Because he couldn't move."

"So why didn't they take him to the hospital?"

"Because it didn't matter anymore. He remained in the shul."

The son understood. "I've coming to Bnei Brak right now," he said.

When he arrived at the shul, Reb Gershon met him outside. "It is not an easy sight. Your father is lying there. I'm not sure you'll be able to take it. Think about whether you want to come in or not."

The son said he did want to go inside, and when he saw his father lying there, he burst into sobs and asked what to do.

"Your father had the great merit to die in the synagogue, wrapped in a tallis, and to not have his body be taken to Abu Kabir on Shabbos. I think it was his wish not to delay the burial."

The son consulted his brother, and they both said to Reb Gershon, "We trust you. Do as you think best."

Within minutes, Toda'ah's loudspeakers were announcing the funeral, saying it was a mitzvah to attend, and within an hour, thousands of people were walking along Rabbi Shach Street to the corner of Jabotinsky, where two buses and private cars waited to take them to the Segula Cemetery.

And so Reb David ended his life with fulfillment of his deepest wish ever since he'd been a concentration camp prisoner—to have a Jewish burial, to merit a respectable funeral, and for there to be a minyan to say Kaddish for him.

This is the special story of Kol Yaakov Synagogue and the late Reb David Weiss, and if you want, you can hear the details from the one who made it all happen. As I told you at the beginning of the story, Reb Chaim, you know him well. I'm talking about your in-law, Harav Gershon Huminer, *shlita*, *rosh yeshivah* in Siach Yitzchak and one of the founders of the Torah-disseminating organization Toda'ah.

A Sack of Banknotes

Rabbi Chaim Zayed, Rabbi of Pardes Katz, is one of People Speak's heroes. This time, he's going to Haifa with a sack full of money.

It goes without saying that he'll come back with a story. But this story is one of the most surprising—and heartwarming—you've ever read.

The story I want to tell is one of the funniest stories I've ever heard and is told by one of your great heroes, Rabbi Chaim Zayed, the rabbi of the Pardes Katz neighborhood, a man who travels the length and breadth of the country giving talks and lectures. Along the way, fabulous stories are drawn to him as if to a magnet, stories which he then recounts in his lectures where they impact ever-wider circles.

About six months ago, Rabbi Zayed married off his daughter. Together, both sets of parents committed to buying basic appliances for the couple, such as a refrigerator, stove, washing machine, and air conditioner, plus essential furniture. After looking in a few stores, they finally found a place that wasn't a real store but a house in Bnei Brak converted into a store, where they found prices for the package that were cheaper than anywhere else, only twenty thousand shekels.

The owner told them straight out that he would deliver the goods to the young couple's apartment only after he was paid in full. And since some things had to be ordered, time was short.

Rabbi Zayed is a busy man, and somehow this task kept getting pushed to the back burner.

A week before the wedding, the store owner called him up. "You might have a problem with your order because if I don't get the money by tomorrow," he said, "I don't see how the young couple will have a refrigerator and air conditioner by their wedding day."

"I'll bring you the money tomorrow, *b'ezras Hashem*, come what may."

"It's up to you," said the store owner said, and ended the conversation.

Rabbi Zayed consulted his planner and saw that he was scheduled to give a lecture in Haifa at ten thirty the following morning.

"I'll go to the bank at eight-thirty right when it opens," he told himself, "withdraw the money and take a taxi to the store. From there, I'll continue on to Haifa, and if all goes well, *b'ezras Hashem*, I'll arrive by ten thirty."

At eight thirty the next morning, Rabbi Zayed was first in line at the bank. He walked up to the counter and asked the teller to give him twenty thousand shekels in cash.

"No problem," the teller said. "But you'll need to wait fifteen minutes for the safe to open."

"I don't have fifteen minutes," Rabbi Zayed told her. "I've got a taxi waiting outside for me. I need to bring the money to someone and then go to Haifa to give a lecture."

The teller sympathized but told him that the bank vault had an automatic mechanism that opened only fifteen minutes after it was activated. Aside from commiserating, there wasn't much she could do.

"Do you have twenty thousand shekels cash that's not in the safe?" Rabbi Zayed asked.

"No, sir, I don't have twenty thousand shekels in cash outside the safe. The whole purpose of the safe is to protect large sums like that."

"So, what am I going to do?" Rabbi Zayed asked in despair.

"Sir?" the teller at the next window called over. "I have twenty thousand shekels here in my cash drawer."

"Great. Then can I come over to you?"

"Sure," said the other clerk. "But you might want to know that the whole twenty thousand is in twenty-shekel bills."

Both clerks burst out laughing.

Rabbi Zayed didn't find it funny. He needed a refrigerator and at least one air conditioner in the young couple's apartment on the wedding day, if possible. If he didn't bring the money that very day, it wouldn't be happening. He added one and one, or maybe twenty and twenty, and said to himself, "A twenty-shekel bill is money, too."

"Give me the twenty thousand in twenties," he said.

The smiles froze on the tellers' faces.

"Are you sure?"

"Absolutely. And please make it as fast as possible."

The work of counting began, and within five minutes, Rabbi Zayed exited the bank with a canvas money sack containing one thousand twenty-shekel bills.

He ran out to the taxi (the wait alone cost him one such bill) and said to the driver, "And now, to the store."

When he got to the store, he was surprised to find it closed.

Apparently, electrical appliance stores don't open until ten. Why? Because there's no need for electrical appliances earlier? Who knows? The bottom line was that the store was locked and bolted.

Rabbi Zayed, standing there with his briefcase and canvas money sack containing one thousand twenty-shekel bills, was shocked.

By now, it was nine. He had to leave right then if he hoped to make it to Haifa in time. As it was, he'd probably be a few minutes late for his lecture.

The taxi drove him to the bus station, where he boarded the bus to Haifa with his bag and everything.

"You sure you don't want to put that sack in the baggage compartment?" the driver asked him.

"I think it's best if it stays with me," Rabbi Zayed said. "In fact, I'm positive."

He took a seat and settled in for the ride—and made it to Haifa exactly on time for his lecture.

The staff and students wondered about the oversized sack lying at Rabbi Zayed's feet. If he wasn't one of the most fascinating speakers of our generation, most likely it would have stolen their attention.

The lecture went well, and the wandering Jew, Rabbi Zayed with his sack, now had to return to Bnei Brak to bring the pile of banknotes to the store and hope all would go well.

Little did he know what was in store for him.

He decided to take the train from Haifa to Tel Aviv because

on the train, he'd be able to put down the bag and immerse himself in learning on the reserved-seating car, where peace and quiet reign.

On the train, it occurred to Rabbi Zayed that due to the morning rush at the bank, an error might have occurred in counting the money. He decided to check. He took out bundle by bundle and began counting. At first, he was careful to count the money while it was still hidden in the sack, but in no time at all, doing so became impossible. After he'd counted all the packets of cash, he discovered to his satisfaction that there were indeed one thousand twenty-shekel bills. In other words, twenty thousand shekels.

Of course, this activity attracted some attention, though Rabbi Zayed was so busy flipping through bills that he didn't notice.

About an hour and a quarter later, the train arrived at the Azrieli station in Tel Aviv, and Rabbi Zayed got off with his sack and walked toward the exit.

There are security check stations at every train station because they are considered a prime target for enemy agents, and when Rabbi Zayed arrived at the security post, his sack screamed like an explosive that could knock down the three Azrieli Towers one after another.

"Put your wallet, phone, and any metal objects on the conveyor belt and walk through the metal detector," the guard told him.

Rabbi Zayed did as instructed but requested permission to carry the sack as he walked through the metal detector.

"No, sir," the guard said. "That must go on the conveyor belt."

"All right," Rabbi Zayed said. He put everything down and walked through the metal detector.

It beeped.

"Do you have any coins in your pocket?"

Yes. He had some coins. He placed them on the tray and walked through the metal detector again. This time it didn't beep.

He went over to the other end of the conveyor belt to collect everything he'd put on it.

The sack was gone.

"Sir, where's the sack?"

"*Savlanut*," the security guard said. "It'll come through soon."

But what came out next was a backpack and then a handbag and another handbag.

"Where's my sack?!" Rabbi Zayed said.

"Let me check."

The security guard stopped the conveyor belt, and they both began to check it. They looked from both sides, above and below, front and back, but the sack was gone.

"What am I going to do now? There were twenty thousand shekels in that sack!"

The security guard laughed. "Why not ten million?"

"Do you think I'm kidding?"

"Sure I think you're kidding. If there was money in that oversized sack, there must have been at least ten million. You can ask anyone."

"On second thought, you've got a point," Rabbi Zayed said. "But the money inside the sack was in twenty-shekel bills."

The security guard burst out in uncontrollable laughter. "Twenty-shekel bills in a canvas sack?" he said when he could finally talk. "You're a riot, Rabbi. But let people go through now."

In a flash, Rabbi Zayed realized that nothing in the world would convince the security guard that there was even a shekel inside that sack because his story was full of holes. He decided to change his approach.

"It doesn't matter what you believe," Rabbi Zayed said to the guard. "There was a sack, and it disappeared, and I want to know what you're going to do about it."

The firm tone of voice brought the man up sharply. He used his walkie-talkie to summon the chief security officer. When he arrived, he said to Rabbi Zayed, "Let's take a look at the cameras."

The minus-one floor of the Azrieli Towers has a room with cameras that cover every inch of the buildings.

"Tell me what time and in what area," the chief security officer said, "and I'll get back to you."

He came back ten minutes later, his face ashen.

"You might not believe this, but the whole line of the cameras hasn't recorded anything for a day and a half, and we knew nothing about it. We have no way of knowing what happened here."

"What does that mean?" Rabbi Zayed asked.

"That means we have no way of knowing what happened to your sack."

Rabbi Zayed asked a few more questions but gradually realized that he had just lost those twenty thousand shekels. He took the chief security officer's contact info in case he'd need it for a lawsuit or something but realized that the chances of him getting the twenty thousand shekels back were about the same as the chances of anyone believing his bizarre story.

He walked away slowly, deep in thought, wondering about

what had just happened to him. "I've been lecturing all my life about how nothing happens by chance. A Jew does not just lose twenty thousand shekels for no good reason, and certainly not under such strange circumstances. I must think about what I need to fix."

Immediately, the answer came to mind.

A week and a half earlier, at one of his lectures, an engaged girl came up to him afterward and asked him to write a letter of recommendation she could use to raise money for her wedding. "Okay," he told her, but he'd forgotten.

You forgot a poor bride? Now you've gotten what you deserve, Rabbi Zayed thought. He promised himself that as soon as he got home, he'd write the letter of recommendation for that girl.

His thoughts were interrupted by a voice asking, "Are you Rabbi Zayed?"

"Yes, I am."

"I don't believe it!" the man said.

He looked secular, and Rabbi Zayed couldn't figure out how the man knew him.

"You don't understand. My daughter watches your lectures all day. Someone in her class brought them to school, and they became the latest rage. We're not religious, just a little bit traditional, but now her whole class is exchanging Rabbi Zayed CDs."

"Thank you," Rabbi Zayed said, thinking, *At least the day includes some compliments.*

"Do me a favor, Rabbi. Right now, I'm making her a surprise birthday party on the forty-ninth floor. There's a restaurant there. Can you come up for a minute and speak? You have no idea what will happen when you walk in. You've been the main topic of conversation for the past few months. It'll be like bringing her the most famous artist."

I'll go upstairs, Rabbi Zayed decided. *What else can I do?* Most likely, he preferred to push off the moment when he'd have to face his family and tell them the bizarre story that cost him twenty thousand shekels.

In seconds, the elevator shot up to the forty-ninth floor to a restaurant called 2C.

When he walked in, the birthday girl nearly fainted. Her friends were no less excited. Rabbi Zayed said a few words and told a short story (no, not this one). As he left the restaurant, the girl's father ran after him.

"How much do I owe the Rav?"

"God forbid. I won't take a penny from you. But if you want to bring more merit to your daughter, there's a poor bride I'm collecting money for."

The man gave him five hundred shekels.

As Rabbi Zayed left the restaurant, it occurred to him that as long as he was there, he might as well take in the spectacular view—or was it that any activity was better than going home?

He took hold of the coin-operated binoculars, put in a few shekels, and then…

He heard a youth beside him talking on the phone. He didn't pay too much attention to the conversation until he said the following words:

"You hear? In twenty-shekel bills. I'm serious. Twenties!"

Whoa.

Rabbi Zayed got goosebumps.

He made himself as inconspicuous as possible as he

considered his next move. Should he call the police? The guy would run away. What should he do?

The guy ended the call and walked toward the restaurant.

Rabbi Zayed followed him and watched as he sat down at a table. On the table sat a bulky object covered by a coat.

Rabbi Zayed decided to do something about it.

He went over to the Russian security guard and said, "That guy is probably a thief. If he tries to run away, I want you to stop him."

The man panicked. "No, I have no authority. I'm not going to do anything. Leave me alone."

Rabbi Zayed remembered that security guards aren't really security guards the same way locks don't really protect a house. He decided to trust in Hashem and just went right over to the guy.

He sat down across the table from him and said to him, "Do you know me?"

"No, Rabbi. Where would I know you from?"

"You'll know me soon. You know the chief of police? We're related. Right now, downstairs, a few policemen are waiting. The security guard has been updated, but you can get off easily. You have something that belongs to me."

The guy was shocked. "Uh, it's yours? I just saw this bag coming off the conveyor belt, and no one came to take it, so I took it. Actually, I wanted to return it, but I didn't know who to give it to."

Rabbi Zayed lifted up the coat, and the canvas sack was revealed in its full glory. "First, I'll take back the sack," he said, which he did. "Now, I think I should call the chief of police who will give you a certificate of excellence for your thought of returning a lost object. Don't you think so?"

"No, please, Rabbi, don't do this to me," the young man pleaded.

"No problem," said Rabbi Zayed, "but you're going to stay right here with me to listen to a story. You are probably wondering how I got here."

"The truth is, I'm in shock," the young man said. "The cameras, right?"

Rabbi Zayed suddenly realized why there were no cameras: so that it would be clear that everything was from Hashem.

Rabbi Zayed sat and told the young man everything he'd been through that day, and when he came to the part of the theft, he told him, "Do you know what my first thought was? When a Jew gets hit, he has to understand that he made a mistake, because Hashem doesn't give us a blow without reason. I realized immediately what I'd done wrong. I'd forgotten about a poor bride's request, and for that, I was beaten. The minute I took it upon myself to repair the damage, an improbable sequence of events brought me to the forty-ninth floor of the Azrieli tower, and from there to the observation deck, a place I would most likely never have gone to in my life.

"Now, something happened to you, too, which means you need to make a change. Are you willing to go to an Arachim seminar?"

"Sure, Rabbi," the young man told him. "And I want to donate money to this bride. Let it be a *kapparah* for my sins."

He took out five hundred shekels (in hundred-shekel bills) and gave it to Rabbi Zayed. Then he gave the Rabbi his name and phone number, and they went their separate ways.

Rabbi Zayed took the elevator down and took a taxi straight to the electrical appliance store. Totally spent, he put the sack of money on the counter as if it was the most ordinary way in the world to pay for electrical appliances.

The clerk opened the sack, looked at the contents, and asked Rabbi Zayed, "Does the Rabbi feel well?"

Then Rabbi Zayed recalled that while the course of the day had somewhat disrupted everything he knew about life, the rest of the world wasn't used to people paying twenty thousand shekels in twenty-shekel bills.

"Talk to the owner," he whispered in a tired voice. "Maybe he'll agree."

The owner came, and when he saw the contents of the sack, he began to laugh.

"I'm sure there's a story behind this sack," he said. "If the story is good enough, I'll take it. Fair enough?"

"Fine, but I think this story will not only be good enough but will make you give me another discount."

"Not a chance," the store owner said. "I've already gone down on the price."

"Okay. You decide," Rabbi Zayed said and began to tell his story.

When he finished telling the story, all the staff members in the story surrounded him open-mouthed.

"The extra discount I asked for is not for me," Rabbi Zayed told the storeowner, "but for the poor bride, and now it's for you to decide how much this story is worth."

The shopkeeper took fifty bills of twenty shekels and gave them to Rabbi Zayed. "This is for the bride," he said. "Mazel tov to you and mazel tov to her, and thanks for the amazing story."

Rabbi Zayed returned home, and the first thing he did was write the bride the letter of recommendation she's asked for. He called her home, apologized profusely for the delay, and asked her to come over right away.

When she arrived, Rabbi Zayed gave her the letter of recommendation and said, "I've already collected some money for you."

He took out the two thousand shekels he'd gotten that day from the father of the girl whose birthday it was, the thief, who was on his way to doing *teshuvah*, and the electronics store owner, sure he'd never found any story as "electrifying."

One Woman to Another

A young teacher becomes a housewife because she feels the teaching profession isn't right for her.

She heads in another direction—and encounters someone from her past. And from that moment on, their paths will intertwine repeatedly.

A visitor to the Shaare Zedek emergency room one night two years ago would have seen two women—one, an emergency room nurse, the other not wearing any uniform—exclaiming in delighted surprise and hugging each other. You couldn't have known what was behind the moving scene. That's what I'm here to tell you.

I think my story, aside from it being a major part of my own life, will resonate with people, especially those who feel stuck. You know, like their future is behind them and there's nothing on the horizon to look forward to.

I married at the age of nineteen, when I was still learning how to teach. I had a very part-time job plus a few hours of tutoring. There wasn't much of an income from it, and certainly not enough.

My husband and I both wanted him to sit and learn, which meant I had to bring in some income. I worked hard and did my job well but it took a lot out of me and didn't really fulfill me the way it does those who feel at home in the profession.

The few hours of classroom time I'd been given went well. My personal integrity didn't allow me to give it less than my utmost. I couldn't see myself getting paid for something I didn't do to the best of my ability.

As part of my work, seminary girls came to observe my classes. Some teachers are bothered by their presence—either because they don't feel comfortable teaching under scrutiny or because it means they need to put in more effort. After all, one hour of teaching a sixth-grade class of girls can't be compared to teaching that same group of girls in front of a group of twenty-year-old observers who dissect your every utterance as well as your ability to maintain class discipline.

By the way, for some teachers, being observed has the exact opposite effect. They like having the seminary students because they enjoy having a more mature audience, and this brings out the best in them (which makes for another point of consideration when thinking about the various ways human beings perceive things).

I viewed it the same way I viewed teaching: a "must" that had to be done well. The lessons I gave included within them my intent to teach the seminary girls as well.

And here's where a young girl named Efrat enters the picture.

She was a gentle girl and very insecure. I could see it on her face.

Right after the first class, I called her for a private conversation, something I hadn't done before with seminary students.

"I see that you're a little insecure," I said.

She was shocked. "How can you tell?"

"Every person knows how to identify his own character traits," I answered without thinking.

"Come on," she responded. "You're full of self-confidence."

"Just the way I want you to be," I said. "Forget whatever you feel. I'll tell you how to overcome it."

From that moment on, I guided her not only during observation of my class but regarding her classwork and tests. I gave myself permission to tell her about myself and that I didn't really see myself as suited to the profession. When she said she felt the same way, I said to her, "Don't waste any time. Go to a professional career counselor to find out what's right for you."

The school year ended and with it the observation by seminary girls. Our relationship came to an end.

She called me up right before Rosh Hashanah and said, "I owe you a big present." Of course, I told her there was no need, and that her statement was a gift in itself, and that was how our brief acquaintance ended. She was busy with her life and I with mine.

My husband was offered a position at his yeshivah, which he took. As things went, since I hadn't enjoyed teaching and since I'd anyway had to search high and low for even part-time positions, I found myself out of work. Unlike many women who are happy to be housewives, it didn't seem to suit me and I soon began to feel very frustrated.

That frustration didn't just spring up on me in one day. It was something that crept up on me over the years, like a hole that deepened an inch every day. You only catch on to what's happening when you're deep in the pit, and then it's hard to climb back out.

I felt bad about myself. I felt I was less than other people—unsuccessful. This was my own personal feeling. I know there are many women who would prefer to be a housewife, but as we said, everyone and his personality. My personality needed to do something besides housework.

Eight years passed. Then things got really bad for me, so I went to a life coach, someone who was supposed to infuse me with renewed energy. After two meetings she told me the following: "You're actually a talented woman and you could be anything you want, in management, teaching, or administrative work. I don't have much to tell you. Just embrace your life, and get professional training in something you'd like to do."

"How? What?" I asked her. "Just start over in the middle of my life?"

"Take it one step at a time. That's it. Everything will follow from that, G-d willing."

I went to a psychologist who specializes in helping people find their ideal career. After several meetings and tests, she told me, "You need a profession related to helping people, like a social worker or something in medicine, a nurse for example."

"How did you know?" I heard myself say to her. "I've wanted to be a nurse ever since I was a kid."

"So why didn't you pursue that as a career?" she asked.

"Come on," I said. "It takes years of study and you need to know all the medications and everything."

"It's not so many years," she said. "Four years at the most, during which you can already begin to work in stages."

"You call that not so many years?" I said with a smile.

"What's the alternative? Keep digging your pit deeper? It will last ninety years. I think four years are not a bad compromise at all."

What do you think? I decided to sign up for nursing school.

I contacted the nursing school. It turned out to be the last day before registration ended.

I had credits to make up (since I'd attended seminary and not a secular program), and I applied myself to the task. I began my studies with zero expectations. I asked myself, *What are the chances that I can climb this mountain?*

To my astonishment, I scored high on test after test, and graduated with honors, with a 95 average.

Then I went to enroll in Shaare Zedek's nursing school.

I was told it was hard to get accepted there, that only one in fifty made it and that each one of them had my ranking.

What were the chances?

I arrived to register. I went to the office and sat down to wait, but the clerk said, "I'm busy. Please go to the opposite counter. She'll attend to you."

I go there, and who do I see?

Efrat.

"What are you doing here?" we both asked simultaneously.

I told her I'd decided to do something I really wanted to do.

"And what are you doing here?" I asked again.

"I also decided to do what I really want," she said. "I started teaching but it didn't work out for me. What you said kept playing through my mind. Finally, I left and did something about it. I consider this job just a stepping stone to what I really want to do."

We sat together and filled out forms, and in between she asked, "How's your English?"

"Not so great," I said. "You caught me."

"They'll catch you, too," she warned me. "You can't pass without knowing English reasonably well."

"So what should I do?" I asked.

"Just take the tests and we'll see," she replied.

I took the tests. I did well on all of them except for English, which I failed miserably.

That was supposed to be the end of my dream. I realized that and so did Efrat. I knew I was going back to my pit.

But I was mistaken. Efrat understood the exact opposite. She approached the administration, who apparently thought highly of her, and vouched for me.

"I observed her classes as a seminary student," she told them. "I am what I am today because of her. She's got personality, she's smart, she has a strong work ethic. She'll close the gap, but she must be here."

Those words got me into nursing school despite all odds.

I began taking courses.

I started "pharmaceutical math." The passing grade on the test is 100. If you fail, you can't continue.

I got 100.

We studied chemistry. Next to me sat a brilliant Russian woman who'd studied chemistry at the university level. You didn't need 100, just a passing grade.

When the results came back, she told me proudly, "I got an 85. How about you?"

Uh-oh. If she got an 85, what were my chances of even passing?

I didn't get the same grade as she did. I got a 97.

It's important for me to mention that right after I began classes, Efrat was promoted to director of a prestigious department at Shaare Zedek. It was obvious that her temporary job as a secretary was Heaven-sent to give me the opportunity to enroll.

We kept up our connection. Not as close friends, but as part of a team of thousands of employees. Almost every time I saw her, I'd say, "I owe you a present."

"What for?"

"Because of you, I'm going to be a nurse," I'd reply.

"Come on," she'd say. "No present necessary. Besides, I'm the one who owes you a present."

And then both of us forgot all about it.

Eventually, I became a registered nurse. From a pale shadow of a woman stuck in a dark pit I became a happy, contented, respected and admired woman. I felt that my children benefited as well. I even read an article about it, that children of working mothers who are happy with their work receive no less than children with an ever-present stay-at-home mom.

The premise of the article was that children of a stay-at-home mom must receive more attention and parental presence than children where both parents work outside the home. Yet the researchers found that mothers who work outside the home and feel fulfilled have something that compensates for their absence and makes them equivalent to the mothers who are at home.

One thing is clear to me: it saved my children. The studies

compared happy housewives with mothers who work outside the home, but I was a very unhappy housewife. A mother like that can find it hard to give of herself to her children, because she feels empty inside and doesn't feel like she has any self to give.

Seven years went by. During that time I was promoted to emergency room nurse. It's a very sensitive, high-pressured job that requires special skills.

One night, an elderly woman was brought by ambulance to the emergency room. She'd fallen and broken her pelvis.

It happens to a lot of seniors. They fall out of bed or in the bath, break bones, and sometimes it starts a downward slide into difficult health situations.

Still, this is not considered an urgent case. Everyone understands why. Breaking a bone is nothing like a heart attack, a stroke, or even trouble breathing.

She was given a bed, and I came to take her blood pressure. As I always do with patients whenever possible, I talked to her. She spoke and sounded lucid. I asked how she had fallen, and she said she'd felt weak and suddenly fell.

These are ordinary things. However, I noticed that she was touching her side as she spoke about the weakness that overcame her.

"Where did you feel the weakness?" I asked, and she said, "Here, and it's very painful."

I looked and immediately called out to the staff, "I want a CT scan of the intestines. I have a feeling something is wrong."

She was transferred to take the CT scan, and it turned out that her fall wasn't just a fall. She had a perforation of the bowel.

Gastrointestinal contamination is a medical emergency that

requires immediate medical attention. It puts the patient in a life-threatening situation, since the contents of the gut spill into the abdomen, which can cause a dangerous infection.

The pelvic fracture had drawn the doctor's attention away from this life-threatening situation. The woman was taken into emergency surgery. The doctors praised me for my vigilance, and I continued my work.

What happened next is this.

The elderly woman's children arrived at the hospital and waited for the surgery to end. Meanwhile, they went to the emergency room to find out what had happened, and one of the doctors told them that the first diagnosis was a pelvic fracture, but that thanks to a nurse's alertness, her life was saved.

I was busy with a patient. A curtain hid me. I heard them talking and knew what was going to happen. They would ask who I was and then shower me with kind words of gratitude. Moments like that give a good feeling to everyone in the medical profession.

Then I heard one of them say, "Can I talk to her? Thank her?"

"Certainly," the doctor said. "She's with a patient right now. She'll come out to speak with you in a few minutes."

A minute later I went out to them, and then I saw her.

"I don't believe it," we both said.

The elderly woman's daughter was Efrat.

It was too incredible to be true.

No one there knew why we fell into each other's arms and cried with joy. Both of us kept saying, "This is unbelievable!"

Everyone waited for us to explain what was going on. I was the first one to calm down.

"You're going to find this hard to believe," I said, "but if it wasn't for Efrat, I wouldn't be a nurse. I'm here because of her. I still owe her a gift for it."

"You just gave me the greatest gift I could ever get," Efrat replied. "You saved my mother's life. The doctors told us that their diagnosis was 'fall and pelvic fracture,' but you sensed that there was something more—and you still think you owe me a gift?"

Efrat and I are now even in terms of gifts, but this story, and especially the good things caused by our wonderful connection, has made us close friends, a kind of living example of the familiar concept: "From one woman to another."

Unlocking the Gates

Rabbi Yaakov Kletzkin is a Yerushalmi chazzan in New York.

That may sound like the beginning of a joke, but the story about him is one of tears, not laughter.

On Yom Kippur of all days, he became engulfed in a quarrel between two congregants that ended in the terrible humiliation of one of them, right at Neilah.

What kind of story can come out of such a story?

You'd be surprised.

I'm a resident of New York. Although I was born in Israel, I've lived in America for over forty years and am a big fan of your stories.

This year there was an incident in our synagogue that reminded me of your stories. There's also a connection with an Israeli living in Bnei Brak.

I daven in a well-known synagogue in Boro Park, Forty-Fifth

Street, at the corner of Fourteenth Avenue. You might even say it's the Itzkowitz of Boro Park.

The synagogue has two floors. On the upper floor, there is a huge synagogue that holds hundreds of people, while the ground floor is for the *shtiblach*, the main one of which holds about one hundred and twenty people. That's where I usually daven.

In recent years, a man by the name of Yaakov Kletzkin has served as our chazzan for the Yamim Tovim. A born-and-bred Yerushalmi now living in Bnei Brak, he travels to us yearly. He and another man who's a veteran davener here are the main protagonists of this story.

For the past ten years, this same veteran davener has bought *pesichah d'Neilah*, opening the ark for Neilah on Yom Kippur, which is considered to bring blessings. Since everyone realized that he was set on buying this honor, the congregants kept bidding the price up until it reached the point where *pesichah d'Neilah* cost two thousand dollars, the same as *maftir Yonah*—and sometimes even more.

A year ago, a dispute arose between that man and the gabbai.

I won't go into detail, but the argument escalated to the point of fury, with talk of open rebellion against the gabbai. People took sides, and attempts were even made to remove the gabbai from his position.

Most of the regulars had no idea how to handle this quarrel. It was bad for everyone, but in America, if it's not your business, you don't get involved. Besides, there were plenty of people who thought it *was* their business, so there was no need for volunteers.

Anyway (as you like to say), Yom Kippur arrived. The same man got ready for the bidding for *pesichah d'Neilah*, but for some reason, the bidding didn't take place.

He asked a few people about it, but they were just as clueless as he was. He couldn't ask the gabbai because they hadn't spoken to one another for a year. He sent a few people to the gabbai, who told them, "Everything's going to be okay. You'll see." They took that as reassurance, returned to the man, and whispered in his ear, "Most likely, he wants to reconcile with you and give you *pesichah d'Neilah*."

Not that this man wanted to reconcile, but what they said reassured him somewhat. He decided that he would first accept the honor of *pesichah d'Neilah* and then notify the gabbai that he couldn't be bought for two thousand dollars and that he'd pay for the honor in full. Then again, maybe he would accept it for free. It didn't really matter. The main thing was to get the honor, which meant so much to him.

The time for Neilah arrived. We all davened fervently. The congregation ended the Shemoneh Esrei, and everyone waited in suspense for the moment the gabbai would call up the man to accept the important honor.

The gabbai finished his prayer and began to walk toward this man, but instead stopped two rows in front of me and signaled another man to step forward.

Most people still didn't realize what was happening. They thought the gabbai was asking someone to call the regular congregant, with whom he wasn't on speaking terms, to honor him with *pesichah d'Neilah*.

But to everyone's shock, the second congregant went straight to the ark, pulled aside the *paroches*, and instructed the chazzan, Rabbi Yankele Kletzkin, to begin the chazzan's repetition.

Rabbi Kletzkin didn't know what was going on. He was

used to the regular congregant, but because he wasn't involved in the matter and didn't even know about the conflict between the man and the gabbai, he thought that this time someone else must have purchased the honor. He began the chazzan's repetition.

There were a few seconds of stunned silence. Everyone was in shock. The chazzan felt that he was carrying the prayer alone, and it was only then that the regular congregant awoke from his shock and began to shout at the man who had opened the *paroches*.

"Thief! Shame on you! Why did you steal my *pesichah*?"

At first, the man who had opened the ark didn't respond but seeing the irate man approaching him with a threatening expression, he said, "I didn't steal it. I bought it yesterday for three hundred dollars. The gabbai sold it to me."

"You sold it to him?!" the affronted man yelled at the gabbai. "Shame on you. You caused the shul a loss of seventeen hundred dollars because of your pettiness!"

Some congregants went over to him and tried to calm him down. "It's Neilah now. It's wrong to shout like that."

"And what he did to me is right? That's what he does to me at Neilah?" he shouted. "You're telling me to not make a ruckus? Kamtza and Bar Kamtza destroyed Jerusalem because the people there kept quiet!"

The chazzan faltered in his prayer, then suddenly stopped and turned around. You could see on his face how shocked he was. His eyes were filled with tears.

Something in his look made everyone fall silent.

He continued his prayer. The congregant who felt he'd been robbed began to wander around the *bimah* sobbing. It was *davka* his heartfelt sobs and not his screams that made each of us feel that it was our business.

Anyone who was even somewhat G-d-fearing realized that this wasn't the way Neilah is supposed to look. And perhaps even worse, it showed the soon-to-be-locked Heaven what kind of people there are in this world, what kind of congregants there are in our little synagogue. Each of us understood that such a spectacle coming to Heaven might bring a flood of terrible troubles to us all. It made us all daven harder, but each of us felt that as long as the man stood there near the *bimah* crying and protesting the insult, no prayer could help us.

Rabbi Kletzkin tried to lift us all on his wings of prayer, but we could all see that his prayer wasn't flowing smoothly. His sweet voice, with its trills, suddenly sounded tired, and he sometimes even lost the melody. It was clear that he felt what was happening behind him and could not daven as usual. We'd chosen Rabbi Kletzkin as our chazzan in the first place because we felt he was not a regular chazzan who just came to do a job, but was completely one with his *tefillah*. This Neilah showed us just how very connected he was when we saw how hard it was for him to connect.

I'll never forget that Neilah. Even the shofar sounded weaker. We all had a terrible feeling.

The prayer ended. As everyone rushed out to go home, Rabbi Kleztkin came over to me and asked for the man's address.

"Why do you want it?" I asked him. "What happened has nothing to do with you, and you're not to blame. It's an internal affair here. Let's eat something to break the fast."

"Not only will I not break the fast," he said, "but in a few hours, I have a flight from Newark Airport, and I don't intend to leave until I settle things. I'm a chazzan and consider myself responsible for the prayer being accepted and bringing good to the entire congregation. But when I consider what happened here earlier, I'm afraid that this prayer wasn't accepted. I'll go to him and obtain his forgiveness of the gabbai and all the other congregants."

I gave him the address, which was a quarter of an hour's walk away, and he ran, still in his slippers and tallis, toward the congregant's house.

I decided to join him. To help him.

We reached the house. A daughter opened the door and said, "My father is sleeping."

What Jew sleeps fifteen minutes after Yom Kippur ends? We told her to ask her mother to tell him we were waiting for him.

Five minutes later, he arrived in the living room. I sat on the side as Rabbi Kletzkin conducted the conversation.

"Listen, Reb Yid (he called him by name). I understand what happened. What they did to you was terrible. But you know something, the grudge you are holding has great significance. I feel like my prayer was blocked."

Those were his exact words.

"I will never forgive him!" the man thundered. "Or the others there. They should have stopped it. Not let me stand there bleeding."

"You're right," Rabbi Kletzkin replied patiently. "I assure you that I too am very angry with the gabbai for doing that to you. And I'll tell you the truth, I actually considered stopping the davening to protest. I said to myself, 'This *tefillah* is a rabbinic ordinance, but *bein adam l'chaveiro* is a Torah injunction.' A few more seconds and I would have done it, but by then, the congregation had already done something, and I felt that they were standing up for you."

The man was very excited about this. "I'm very surprised that you came here, and I'm very touched that care about me to such an extent. Hold on a minute." He ran to a nearby room and came back with three hundred and fifty dollars and tried to give it Rabbi Kletzkin.

"I won't take the money," Rabbi Kletzkin said, "and soon I'm going to miss my flight. I'm worried about the *tefillah* and the *kahal*. It was a public prayer, *tefillah shel tzibbur*, and you, too, are part of that *tzibbur*. I'm asking you to overcome your feelings of anger and to forgive."

The man fell silent. He seemed to wage an inner battle before saying, "Do you know why I buy *pesichah d'Neilah*? I have two unmarried children, one thirty-seven and the other thirty-five. I've been buying *pesichah d'Neilah* for the past ten years so that in its merit, my children will find their *zivug*. Do you think this gabbai robbed me of the *honor*? He robbed me of my children's *shidduchim*!"

He began to cry, wrenching, choking sobs. Roars of sorrow that filled the whole house. It was terrible.

Rabbi Kletzkin waited. He didn't say a word but shed tears along with the man. He felt close to him, as did I.

He waited for the crying to subside and then told him, "I want to tell you a story from the *Zohar* in *parashas Miketz*."

This is what he said.

Rabbi Aba sat at the gate of the city of Lod. He saw a man sitting on a small outcrop of a hill. The man was so tired from his travels that he fell asleep right where he sat. While he was sleeping, Rabbi Aba saw a snake going toward him. A reptile came out and killed the snake. When the man woke up, he saw the dead snake. The man stood up, and the hill then collapsed into the valley below. He was saved. A moment later, and he would have been killed by the landslide.

Rabbi Aba came to him and said, "What have you done to deserve these two miracles that Hashem did for you—because these events did not happen by chance."

The man said, "I always forgave and made peace with anyone who did evil to me. And if I couldn't make peace, I didn't go to sleep without forgiving him and all those who hurt me. Even more, from that day on, I tried to do them good."

Rabbi Aba cried and said, "This man's actions are greater than those of Yosef. Those who wronged Yosef were his brothers. He would certainly have pity on them. But what this man did is greater, and so he is worthy of having God make miracle after miracle for him."

"That's the story," Rabbi Kletzkin said. "And now, listen to me. This *segulah* of *pesichah d'Neilah* hasn't helped you. Maybe it worked for other people, but not for you. I suggest you try a much more powerful *segulah* so that your children will get married this very year: Forgive completely the gabbai, forgive completely everyone in shul—and you'll see, *b'ezras Hashem*, great salvations."

The man was silent. You could see that Rabbi Kletzkin's words made a big impression on him.

After a few moments of silence, he said, "So what do I have to do?"

"Just say three times 'So-and-so (he said the gabbai's name) is *machul* (forgiven) and everyone in the shul is *machul*.' Mean it with all your heart, and God-willing, you'll see that your prayers will be answered."

The man said *machul* three times with the name of the gabbai and the congregation, and then the three of us stood up and broke into a joyous dance. Rabbi Kletzkin rushed to his lodgings and from there left for the airport.

And now we reach the dramatic end of the story.

Two months later, the thirty-seven-year-old eldest son got engaged.

Two months after that, the second son got engaged.

By Pesach, both were married.

The man no longer davened in our synagogue, for reasons he kept private. But to the gabbai and the rest of us, it was as clear as day what had caused the double miracle for that congregant.

I'm not saying that the insult was sent from Above to bring him to forgiveness. The insult remains an insult. A terrible thing happened in our synagogue, something for which we could have all paid a steep price. The Gates of Heaven were locked before us, and that last thing that happened was something not even Yom Kippur cannot atone for.

But after Neilah came the hope, thanks to the unexpected forgiveness, which I believe caused He Who sits On High to laugh, to forgive the gabbai and the congregants, and to give the man who forgave the biggest of all presents—real *Yiddishe nachas* from his two sons who'd had a very hard time finding their mates.

Here in New York, I long for Rabbi Yaakov Kletzkin's return. As you and everyone reading this story have discovered, he's not only a chazzan but a great Jew with a great soul who succeeded with his wisdom and good *middos* in steering an entire community away from a bad decree to good news and a good year.

VIP Treatment from Above

A young girl suddenly loses her father, and her world is destroyed.

She's worried not only about herself but about her nine siblings. Who will take care of them?

The story answers this question in a very special way.

Consider it a gift to orphans everywhere.

For years now, I've been planning to send my story to you, but life is so busy. A week goes by and then another, and every so often, I remember this special story that's perfect for you and your readers.

It starts like all stories, but instead of "one sunny day," it begins, "One dark night." Literally.

One dark night, my parents and I were sitting in the living room after an especially busy day. I was seventeen at the time, the eldest of ten children. I sat there with my notebooks and class notes, almost finished with my homework, just waiting for the minute I could go to sleep.

My mother, tired after a hard day's work and taking care of the children, sat in an armchair, sipping a cup of coffee and reading the daily newspaper. My father sat at the head of the table, bent over a large Gemara with several open *sefarim* nearby, learning in a soft, pleasant melody.

People don't know how grateful they should be for a blessed routine. They just go about living their lives, never thinking that in one instant everything could change. No one prepared me for what happened next.

The silence that was suddenly broken made me and my mother jump. We heard a choking gasp from Abba's direction. The scene that met my eyes was unbearable.

My father's head was slumped on the Gemara, and his hand gripped his heart in pain. The screams that came out of our mouths weren't planned, and I can't remember exactly who called Hatzalah. What I do remember is that within minutes, the living room was filled with the din of Hatzalah and Magen David Adom responders, medical instruments, beeps, and walkie-talkies. They lay my father on the floor, and everyone clustered around him.

One moment, in particular, stands out in my memory, never to be forgotten. That was when the man who had been working on my father for about twenty minutes lifted up his hands as if to say, "It's over."

So. The house filled with dozens of people—aunts and uncles, friends and neighbors.

They were talking about a funeral, a grave, shivah.

What scary concepts. Maybe it was all a bad dream.

I also heard neighbors dividing up the childcare as if the children were objects ("Moishie will be by you. I'll take Chanie and Rivky").

There were arguments between the uncles about how to notify Savta, Abba's mother, who'd been widowed herself almost a year earlier.

That was it. Life stopped.

There was life before Abba died, and life after. Period.

In the morning, before the funeral, my homeroom teacher arrived. She was someone I really admired.

I was very embarrassed. I'm such a good student that teachers had never needed to reach out to me. Besides, I didn't need anyone from there, not even friends. All I wanted was to be left alone with my family.

Actually, what I wanted most was Abba!

The teacher must have been instructed not to pay attention to my frosty facial expression because she deliberately ignored it.

She cleared a room where we could talk privately, directed me into it, and we both sat on the bed.

She was smart. She didn't try to get me to talk, and she didn't smile at me. She just held a book in her hand, the *Kitzur Shulchan Aruch*, and said softly to me, "There are halachos that aren't studied in seminary because we hope they'll never be needed. But here we are. Let's look together at the halachos of shivah.

We sat and studied. She read each halachah, explained it, and continued.

When we'd finished, she said, "Elisheva, I was also orphaned at a young age. My mother passed away, and I married off all my brothers and sisters." Then she started telling me how she coped. (I was in shock! This special, revered teacher, an orphan?)

"I want you to know that now that your father is upstairs," she said, "he can help you even more than when he was here. And the Father of Orphans is your own personal Father! Turn to Him at all times! Because orphans get VIP treatment from Above."

At the time, I didn't know that her words would accompany me for many years.

My thoughts in those moments were about who would take Aharon to shul, who would help Eliezer learn for his Gemara test, who would preside over our Shabbos table (how painful it was just to think of it! Tears of longing ran down my cheeks). How would we have money? Who would smile at us and make us laugh, who would listen to us, guide us, and tell us inspirational stories? Who would set the Shabbos clock, and who would repair the clock for us when it broke?

I was also thinking about how my mother would be alone and wondering who she'd share her life with now.

I also thought about little Chanie, who was just beginning to say the word "Abba." I thought it was such a shame that she wouldn't remember him at all.

I also thought about Succos, Pesach, and Shavuos. Enough! Abba, can you please come back?

I'm going to fast forward now, skipping over the long years of my childhood, which were full of ups and downs, hard days, and those less so. Days of longing and days of joy, days of immense loss, and days of imagining what would be if Abba were still here.

The years passed. I married a wonderful man, *baruch Hashem*. One by one, my brothers and sisters got married too. Only my little sister remained at home, and she wasn't that little anymore but a grown girl ready to get married. My mother had begun to enjoy her *nachas* and could take things a bit easier after the busy and complex years of raising us all.

Each time, I was thrilled anew with how the words of that teacher proved true and how much strength they gave me. All the *shidduchim* came about with such amazing *siyatta diShemaya*. You can ask any orphan or widow, and they'll tell you how they feel with certainty that Someone up there is helping things along.

Only my little sister, Chanie, was left. Somehow, with her, things got stuck. Us older sisters got married relatively quickly, but for some reason, she still hadn't found the right one.

I couldn't help but think of what the teacher had said. I began to daven to Hashem and also talk to my Abba in Heaven about getting me some VIP service in this matter. Isn't that what they promised me?

Seemingly unrelated to this story, a woman in a distant city who came from an illustrious family that belongs to our *chassidus*, passed away after a serious illness. She and her husband had married off all but one of their children: a young man with a now brokenhearted, despondent father.

They began receiving *shidduch* suggestions. My sister's name was among them.

The brokenhearted father was not emotionally available to consider *shidduchim* for his son right then. It only reminded him of how carefully his righteous wife, *a"h*, had looked into each suggestion. He couldn't imagine himself stepping into those shoes.

Naturally, the matchmakers persisted and pressured until the father called his eldest daughter (who was marrying off her own children), and said he would be sending all the matchmakers—and their pressure—to her.

The eldest daughter was reluctant. It pained her to have her mother's position given to her.

Now she got the phone calls, wrote down names, rejected them, and in the meanwhile, made no progress.

As time went by, the urgency faded, and the boy's status remained as it was.

It would soon be time for the *yahrtzeit*, and the family planned to visit the grave on Har Hazeisim. Since they lived far away, they decided to hire a large van to go together and daven at their gravesite of their illustrious mother, *a"h*.

On the designated day, the van arrived, and everyone boarded silently. The driver, who was not religious, sensed the mood and didn't play any music. Along the way, everyone was busy saying *tehillim*, thinking deeply and with great pain at how unbelievably fast a year had flown by since they'd parted from their mother.

When they reached their destination, they started to get out of the van and were surprised to see the driver preparing to exit the van as well. He pulled a folded *kippah* out of the glove compartment, a tiny *sefer Tehillim* from somewhere else, and got out with them.

They were very surprised. Their group had enough people for a minyan, and they didn't know this man. Naturally, they didn't say anything but descended the stairs that led to the section where their mother was buried.

As they approached the grave, they noticed that the driver didn't stay with them but continued on his way. They watched as he stopped next to an older headstone, opened his *sefer Tehillim*, and began praying with deep concentration.

Occasionally, he wiped away a stray tear, still fully concentrating on prayer and supplications.

The family was intrigued. Who was this driver, and who was buried there?

When they finished, the family headed back to the van. They noticed that the driver had finished his prayers and now put his head on the tombstone and wept. He then picked up a stone and reverently placed it on the marble. One last kiss to the headstone, and then he walked away backward, never turning his back on it.

One of the brothers ran quickly to see what was written on the tombstone. He saw that it said, "Rav Shalom." (It was my father, *z"l*, who had passed away twenty years earlier.) This brother told everyone what was written, but no one had a clue as to the driver's connection with the deceased.

When they got back in the van, the driver took off the *kippah* and put it back in the glove compartment. The father of the family, who sat next to him, couldn't help but ask as they drove, "What's your connection to Rav Shalom?"

Everyone listened intently to the driver's response.

"Rav Shalom was a *rosh mesivta* in a yeshivah where I studied in my teens."

I want to interject here that when I was a little girl, we lived for a time in one of the communities in the south of the country.

There, boys from local communities could choose to study in a special school that combined Torah learning with vocational training. The parents usually wanted their children to acquire a profession, but at the same time remain good Jews. My father, *z"l*, was a *mashgiach* or *rosh mesivta* there. I don't remember exactly what his official role was, but he was a highly respected and beloved figure. He became a loving father to everyone, and each boy felt like an only son. He was devoted to them, heart and soul. We lived near the yeshivah but coming home always took him over an hour. He was always surrounded by students who accompanied him with admiration and affection. The whole way home he would speak kindly to them, give them encouragement, and speak words of truth. They would consult with him about their concerns, and he, with his great wisdom and his infinite love, knew how to touch their hearts and give them what they needed. On the way home it was nice to see how, during the conversation, he smiled at one, clapped the shoulder of another so that everyone was satisfied.

I remember running to him, holding his hand with my little one. I would feel the students looked at me with envy as if they wanted to change places with me, jealous that I could be with the Rav all the time.

On Friday nights after the *seudah*, the boys would come to our house and sit until late at night, enjoying the refreshments my mother prepared, singing and rejoicing, and listening to pearls of wisdom from Rav Shalom.

I told you only a small part of his many deeds just to give an introduction to what the driver told us next.

"I grew up in a nonreligious family," the driver continued, "but my parents wanted me to have a religious education.

Rav Shalom put a lot of effort into me and my friends, and we loved him, heart and soul. If there was anyone in my life who really loved me, it was Rav Shalom. I still miss him. I can still picture his big smile and his warm look that told me he believed in me and my ability to succeed.

"Life is not simple or easy for me now. I lived in poverty and deprivation for years until I found a job, and it's not easy work. My family also broke up, and I can barely keep up with the payments that were imposed on me, but with all that, I keep Shabbat, and tefillin and kosher, all thanks to Rav Shalom. Whenever I go through rough times, I recall the only person in the world who trusted me, believed in me, supported me, and loved me. And that was Rav Shalom, *z"l*. Whenever I drive people to Har Hazeisim, I take the opportunity to go to his gravesite and pray for the elevation of his soul."

The passengers sat in stunned silence.

Then, the eldest sister, the one who'd been given the job of finding a good *shidduch* for the youngest brother, bent forward and whispered to her father, "Abba, guess what? Recently someone suggested Rav Shalom's daughter to us."

"Really?" her father said. "Why didn't you tell me?"

"I did tell you, Abba, and you said you'd look into it.'"

"You're right," the father said. "I'll do it right now."

To the driver, he said, "His daughter was just suggested to us as a match for our son."

The driver was so excited he slammed both hands on the steering wheel. "Really? Grab her! Do you know what kind of children Rav Shalom has? How well they were brought up? I'm telling you, I've known them since they were little. Let me tell you about his daughter." (He meant me, the eldest. But what difference does it make? They were all listening eagerly.) "What a wonderful girl, so soft-spoken, such respect for her parents, so pious. Anyone who doesn't take her is losing out!"

Everyone listened in silence as the driver continued to sing the praises of the bride (which she was, as far as he was concerned) and her family and everyone in it.

The eldest sister decided to take matters into her own hands and move the *shidduch* forward. No one there noticed from whom exactly they were getting their information—from a person who was as far away from their circles as could possibly be, someone who had no understanding of the subtleties of matchmaking. But what can you do? When Hashem wills it, anything can happen. And when my father in Heaven wants us to get the VIP treatment, no one can control from where it comes.

Only a week later, they broke the plate, and my little sister got engaged to the boy. Remember, I told you we're chassidim, in case you're wondering why it happened so quickly.

How did we find out this part of the story?

After the wedding, I just happened to ask my sister's sister-in-law how they found out about us and why it took them so long to check us out. After all, the *shidduch* had been suggested half a year earlier.

"A long time?" she said. "Do you consider thirty-four hours to investigate a long time?"

"The suggestion was made six months earlier."

Then she told me what had happened to the suggestion and how it had been revived suddenly and by whom.

I wouldn't dream that a struggling secular driver would be the source of my little sister's match (of course, they confirmed the information elsewhere, and it wasn't all that hard, but still, it was this encounter that catapulted the match to finalize within a week).

Only then did I realize how true my teacher's words were. The circle had closed! From Above, Abba had gotten us VIP treatment, and how!

Today the couple already has three children. May they be blessed with many more and with many years of happiness.

I want to dedicate this story to all the orphans and widows so that they realize that, "You are children of the Lord, your G-d" (*Devarim* 14:1). Hashem forbids us to overly mourn the dead because we believe that the dead do not disappear. Only the body fades away, and the orphans gain a father who is in Heaven, and Hashem as the Father of orphans.

Womanly Wisdom Built Our Home

A young bride marries with dreams of building a wonderful home.

Her dreams are shattered when she finds out her husband's true nature.

As if that's not enough, her mother-in-law interferes.

How likely is it that this home will remain intact?

You'll be surprised to find out, when help comes from the most unexpected source.

I got married twenty-five years ago. I came from a warm, good home. I was considered an outstanding student, and when I began *shidduchim*, I was suggested to top boys.

Finally, a good boy from an excellent—you could even say distinguished—family was suggested. We met, he was smart, eloquent, and impressive, and there was no reason for me not to move forward to an engagement.

So we got engaged.

Already during the engagement period, a few things bothered me. He treated me well, but his attitude toward others gave me a strange feeling. I noticed that he wasn't happy for other people—not his friends, his siblings, not even his parents. It made me uncomfortable, and I was wise enough to realize that someone who couldn't be happy for the people closest to him wouldn't want to see me happy either.

Let me take this opportunity to warn all engaged couples to be very careful to maintain all the usual customs, specifically because of the point I'm raising. The engagement period is a very sensitive time, and people think that if they're nice to their partner, that's enough. But reality isn't like that. Because both partners, if they're not stupid or blind, can discern negative character traits in the other even if they're not directed against them.

If a guy is angry with the waiter when they meet because it took him a while to serve a glass of water, it means he's an angry, impatient person. If a guy is critical of his parents, teachers, and friends, he'll be critical of his wife. And if a girl relates how hurt she was by an offhand remark and draws deep conclusions from it that people are jealous of her and don't want her to have anything good, she reveals the fact that she, as unpleasant as it is to say, suffers from complexes.

I didn't do a thing about these thoughts. Why? Maybe because I didn't want to upset my parents, maybe because I wasn't sure about what I was thinking, or maybe because I just preferred to think that after the wedding I could change him for the better and that it would never be turned against me.

We got married.

A month and a half after the wedding, my concerns were

validated. The boy I married turned out to be very problematic. Like a puzzle slowly revealed, it turned out that he had issues with everyone he came into contact with, and soon enough, it reached me, too.

And I still hadn't told my parents. I just kept it in my heart and felt miserable.

The first time it burst out, it actually came from him. One day, he argued with me about something unimportant, and at one point, he said, "I'm not willing to live like this anymore. I'm going to my parents." And he left.

I sat at home alone, crying. I didn't know what to do. I decided to call my parents and tell them what I was going through.

But before I could place the call, I heard a knock on the front door. I peered nervously through the door viewer and was surprised to see my mother-in-law standing there.

As if what I was going through wasn't enough, now she was there to tell me off. I wasn't sure I should even open the door, but out of common courtesy, I did.

She walked into the living room, sat down, and asked me to sit opposite her.

I sat down.

"Our son came home and said there was a fight between you," she said to me.

"Did he tell you what it was about?" I interrupted her angrily.

"No, he didn't tell us, but I already know who's to blame."

"Really? Without even asking you know who's to blame?"

"Really," she said.

I wanted to end the conversation right then and there, I was so furious. But then I heard her say, "I'm sure it's his fault, not yours."

My breath caught. "Uh, how do you know?"

"Because I know you," she replied. "You're a wonderful girl

with excellent *middos*. A very special girl. I can't believe that I merited such a fantastic *kallah*. You don't have a single flaw. So I don't need to hear the details to know that you're not to blame."

I started to cry. She went to bring me a glass of water and waited patiently until I calmed down.

"My husband and I told him to look for another place to stay. He's not coming back to us, that's for sure. And I suggest that you not let him come back here until he asks your forgiveness."

I couldn't believe what I was hearing. My mother-in-law was taking my side without even finding out what happened. And not only that, she was giving me advice against her son!

"I'm a little confused," I responded. "Why are you working against your son?"

"You tell me," my mother-in-law replied. "If I hadn't come here, how long would it have taken you to go to your parents?"

"I was just about to do that," I admitted.

"And then my son might lose the best wife he could ever have! That's why I rushed over here, hoping that you hadn't left yet. I came to give you our full support, and we hope you will agree to give him another chance. Do you think that's called acting against my son?"

She was so right, but it still seemed strange to me.

She sat there with me, and I told her everything I was going through. She agreed with me on everything, never once saying that I should have acted differently. The opposite. Some of the things I told her made her madder than I was about them, and she said, "You shouldn't have allowed something like this to happen." I couldn't believe what was happening. A mother was sitting there, taking her daughter-in-law's side. As strange as it sounded to me, it gave me the strength and support I so desperately needed.

"Now, this is what we're going to do," she said. And here, she gave me her recipe for how to teach him a lesson and make him apologize and behave better. Then she opened her purse, took out her wallet, and removed a lot of money. "Here," she said, handing it to me. "I want you to go out and buy whatever you want. From now on, if you have any trouble, come to me."

And then she left.

I rubbed my eyes. I didn't believe that such a thing could happen, but her visit certainly lifted my spirits and gave me strength.

He returned several hours later, apologized nicely, and promised never to repeat what he'd done.

But he didn't change. People don't change that fast, especially people who don't think they have any reason to change. Gradually I realized that I'd been had. From the information I gathered, mostly from my husband, I realized that since childhood he was both very smart and hardworking, but emotionally, socially, and personally, he had big problems. His parents took him to all kinds of professionals, but he always blamed them and viewed them as his enemies. Actually, he felt that way not just about them but about the whole world.

When he entered yeshivah, they hoped that would change. And he really did change, because society is less forgiving than parents, and he was smart enough to realize that certain things couldn't be done, and if he did them, only he would pay the price. He had falls here and there, and he paid very heavy prices for them, like having to change yeshivahs. He was a sharp boy, a good learner, and smart, and made sure not to get into trouble. But when he did, the trouble was so bad and so obvious that he couldn't continue at that yeshivah. With his own two hands he destroyed his future at that yeshivah.

Despite the heavy price he paid, he learned nothing. Maybe, just maybe, he'd learned to avoid doing things that would ruin him, but he didn't make any real changes within himself. On the contrary, he walked around like a caged lion and blamed the whole world for his troubles.

Over the years, they told him, "You've got to realize that when you get married, all these things will hit you. You have to make a change. Go to therapy." But all their advice fell on deaf ears.

And he managed to marry someone like me. Sorry that I'm giving myself so many compliments, because it's not that I'm perfect. It's just that I'm a good person with positive intentions, dedication, patience, and good *middos*, and there was no reason for me to get someone who wasn't like me, but it was my fate, and I came to terms with it. That is, not with the behavior, but with the fact that I had to deal with this behavior.

Over the years, it only happened twice that my parents saw what I was going through. That's because most of it took place at home. Both of these times led to my parents doing what was expected of them: They informed me that I was coming home and that things couldn't go on this way.

What surprised my parents, and also made matters work out, was my mother-in-law's incomprehensible behavior.

She talked to my parents, told them they were right and they were doing the right thing, that their daughter was a wonderful person and a wonderful wife, and that she'd support any decision I made; even if I decided to break up the marriage she'd support me and compensate me for all the difficult years.

My parents weren't prepared for this approach. She took them by surprise. This allowed a relaxed conversation to take place. At first, my parents put the blame on my mother-in-law and said that she was a partner in setting the trap I fell into. She didn't deny it. She just said, "He's my son. What would you have preferred, that I lose all hope? First, I thought he would change in yeshivah, and then I hoped that marriage would change him. Please don't judge me."

This was a winning approach, precisely because it was an open declaration of defeat. She was strong only because she didn't have even a drop of power. She was persuasive only because she admitted her mistake. And she was smart precisely because most counselors and advice-givers would have told her to try to put some of the blame on me, to try to justify her son's behavior, and deny she knew he had problems, to claim I was the one who'd ruined his life and all sorts of accusations like that. People might think they're smart, but in the end they cause the greatest damage to themselves and their children.

But not my mother-in-law. All during this period, she didn't say one word to vindicate her son or blame me, though I must admit, at that time, I did some nasty things to him, such as preventing him from seeing the children and demanding support beyond his ability to supply.

My parents were sure she would break at this, but no. She paid me herself what her son couldn't and begged that at least

I would let her see her grandchildren. My parents and I didn't have the heart to say no. Whenever I think of it, I cry. Because those are the only moments I'm a little ashamed of.

Eventually, we reached an arrangement: meetings in her home. I would bring the kids, and my mother-in-law would beg me, "Come on in and have something to eat. You're my daughter. Feel comfortable here." But I said, "We're getting a divorce, so it's not right for me to do that."

She would step outside, shower me with compliments and love, and give me money. Later, she'd send food to my house so that I, too, could eat her delicious cooking.

Her behavior, without any signs of war, softened my parents. And then, for the first time, my husband agreed to go for treatment, which helped a little, even if it didn't change him completely.

We got back together again. One child and then another was born, and on the whole, we were able to build an exemplary family and even marry off two daughters respectably to boys from excellent families. I don't envy them the investigating we did, from the hospital bassinet on....

In your stories, the mother-in-law usually dies at the end, and then the bride tells how special she was, and everyone is crying. I thought about it when I read your story about the father who had treated his rebellious daughter so well. He died suddenly, before she had a chance to tell him she'd become a *baalas teshuvah*, so he left the world without knowing about her decision.

As I read that story and cried like everyone else, I decided I wouldn't wait for something to happen to my mother-in-law; I'd write my story (with slight changes to disguise identities) to pay tribute to her in her lifetime. She deserves it.

It says, "Womanly wisdom built her home." I want you to know, my beloved *shvigger*, that I always think, "Womanly wisdom built *our* home." If not for your wisdom, understanding, and special virtues, our home would have collapsed after a few months—or worse, after a dozen years, with broken children and endless battles that would have destroyed them and future generations. But you were there, and with your good *middos* and womanly wisdom, you built our home and maintained it for so many years.

In *parashas Ki Sisa*, we see that Hashem asks that the man to build the Mishkan not be an engineer or an artist. Rather, He asks for a "wise-hearted man." Only a man who has both wisdom and virtue can build a Mishkan.

And you, my beloved *shvigger*, succeeded in building not only our home but all the homes our children will build for all generations.

Although you are alive and well, *baruch Hashem*, I find myself crying as I write these things. They are tears of emotion and not pain, tears of love and admiration for the mother-in-law I merited to have, and I hope this will inspire all the mothers-in-law of the world.

Baqqashot

A teenager grows up in the shadow of a distant father, in a bad, unfeeling, lonely environment. All signs point to a downward spiral.

Only one thing keeps him from falling completely: baqqashot.

I grew up in a chareidi home, a regular kid in all ways, the seventh of nine children. I was good in secular studies but not in learning.

It took a lot of work, but I finally got accepted into a good yeshivah in Bnei Brak.

In the beginning, everything was okay, but as time went on, I couldn't keep it up. I didn't feel any satisfaction in my learning. I just couldn't find myself.

For me, the worst part was the humiliation. I had a hard time waking up in the morning. The dorm supervisor would wake me up once, and if I didn't get up, he'd flip the mattress over—with me still on it.

One morning when he came to wake me up, I said, "All right already. I'm getting up." And then he just slapped me across the face.

I cried out. Not because of the pain but because of the humiliation. I was devastated. I went to the rosh yeshivah and told him what had happened.

He said he'd check it out.

That afternoon when I went back to him, he said, "I investigated. Isn't it true that you called him a *rasha*?"

"Yes. I said that to him."

"We don't act like that," the rosh yeshivah said. "Go home for a week."

I couldn't believe what I was hearing. "But I had a good reason for calling him that. He slapped me across the face for nothing."

"Go home," the rosh yeshivah told me.

That broke me. And as if that wasn't enough, a week later, the yeshivah notified my parents that they had decided I wasn't a good fit for their yeshivah. To prove their point, they didn't try to find me another yeshivah.

I was thirteen-and-a-half, alone and bored. I started thinking thoughts that are bad for a child to have. Spiritually, I reached new lows. I stopped putting on tefillin, stopped keeping Shabbat, and pretty much dropped everything that's part of a chareidi lifestyle.

It was a horrible feeling, a feeling of terrible emptiness, with no purpose or goal. On the one hand, I felt mature; on the other hand, I was still a child. I decided to become an atheist, but it wasn't really atheism because my decision stemmed from anger.

What I lacked most was moral support.

Instead of support, my father just stopped talking to me.

Not that I'd had a good relationship with my father before this happened. He'd always gotten up to pray with a *neitz* minyan while I'd gone at eight. Any conversation between us was sure to include put-downs and suggestions for my improvement, so I did everything I could not to talk to him, and he never tried to talk to me.

My father was a pretty closed guy; my mother was more open.

A few months later, I went to a different yeshivah, this time in Yerushalayim. But after a week there, when I got into a fight with another kid and we exchanged blows, the *mashgiach* said to me, "You can leave."

The next day I came back anyway. The *mashgiach* pulled me from the front of the *beis medrash*, and in front of everyone pinned me against the wall like some Border Police guard arresting an Arab. I burned with shame and wished the ground would swallow me up.

I spent another period at home after which I entered a different yeshivah. There, too, I couldn't find myself. I was in bad shape. I'd do stupid things, like going into the *mashgiach's* room and calling home, acting as if the call was urgent. Very funny. Who exactly was I going to talk to?

I would take eggs from the yeshivah kitchen and throw them at the wall. I'd break into the office at night, copy a test from the top boy, and then leave. Stuff like that.

Really, I was just a lonely kid who had no relationship whatsoever with his father. I lived in my own world of misery.

I was thrown out of this last yeshivah, too. What else? They got tired of cleaning eggs off the walls and replacing locks. At fourteen-and-a-half, I found myself once again without a framework.

With my father, there were conflicts that even included raised hands. He would wake me up in the morning and start throwing things at me. If I ever brought friends home, he had no problem shouting at me and hitting me in front of them.

At fifteen, I entered a special boarding school. I studied electronics there and maintained my status primarily by doing well in secular subjects.

There, too, however, I had an incident with a teacher. He asked me to leave the *beit knesset* because he thought I was talking. I grabbed him and shouted, "You're not going to tell me to go outside!"

"Okay!" he answered in a panic. "I won't say it! Just let me go."

I let go of him. He didn't respond. One of the guys approached me gently and told me to go outside.

At least I felt that I left with my self-respect intact.

Then guys came to talk with me. I went and apologized to the teacher. That was the first time I'd ever apologized to anyone. Why? Because they approached me as if I was a person, not an insect.

At this school, the staff was skilled at understanding the boys. They understood that we weren't bad but bleeding from open wounds, and these wounds needed to heal, not have salt thrown on them.

At sixteen, I started working at Angel's Bakery in Geulah.

I lived at my parents' house in the center of Yerushalayim. Whenever they annoyed me, I'd play music on Shabbat, and then World War III would break out. My parents would throw things into the room, I'd leave the house, and when I returned, the screams and fights and beatings would start.

One day, when there was a serious struggle, my father called the police. I was taken down to the police station, and the officer demanded, "Sign that you won't go home."

I ripped up the sheet of paper in front of his eyes.

"That's what you're doing to me? I'll show you what's what."

He arrested me. I was sitting in a cell with someone who'd burned an ATM. Why did he do it? Because he felt like it. He was disturbed, like me.

In the morning, they let me go.

"You've got a good father," the policeman spat at me. "He pestered me all night to let you go."

I burst into tears. I don't know why. Maybe because it was the first time I felt my father cared about me.

Because he cared even briefly, I decided to stop giving my parents trouble and rented an apartment for myself.

A kid of seventeen, working and supporting himself. That's what I was.

I didn't exchange a word with my father. My mother wanted me to come home. I'd go home, take a few things, and leave.

I had a probation officer who met with me for hours simply to make himself some money at the government's expense. Nothing good came out of it for me.

My mother begged me to come back home, and one day I did. I still hadn't talked to my father.

I enrolled in night school to get my high school equivalency degree. I completed the course, making deliveries during the day. I made enough money to cover personal expenses but nothing more.

Then I was drafted. If you ask me if the army is good, I'll tell you this: it's not a place for anyone religious.

As low as I had sunk religiously, being in the army was my biggest test, as far as religion went. They said that at least there they'd make a man out of me, but I didn't get along there either.

I was a driver, an easy non-combatant job. Even so I managed to get thrown into military prison three times for skipping guard duty and talking back to the NCO.

Still, I didn't desecrate Shabbat and I put on tefillin every day.

The only thing that connected me to religion were the *piyyutim* and *baqqashot* of Shabbat. I might not pray, but *baqqashot*? As many as possible.

Ashkenazim won't understand the meaning of *piyyutim*, but during all these years, I would listen to all kinds of *paytanim*, and I sang a lot of *piyyutim* to myself.

After the army, I debated whether to study acting or *piyyutim*.

I went to the Nissan Nativ Acting Studio. Fortunately, it was closed. From there, I headed to the Jerusalem Great Synagogue, where they teach *piyyutim*.

Try to understand how confused I was: either acting, a completely secular vocation, or *piyyutim*, all in one day.

I started studying there. I was in first place in their classes both the first and second year (in the second year, seventy percent of the participants dropped out).

They had excellent teachers who worked with us slowly. It took them a whole year to teach us five of the main *maqams*.

For those who aren't familiar with this, a *maqam* is a type of melody based on a scale with notes not found in Western music. There are about ninety-eight *maqams*, the most famous being Ajam and Nahwand. Only Rav Ovadia knew all the *maqams*.

People think the *maqams* come from Arabic music, but the truth is that the Arabs took it from us at the time of the Beit Hamikdash.

During this time, I kept myself in line. Shabbat, tefillin, *tzniut*.

Friends made suggestions, but I wanted a good girl.

"Look at you," they'd say to me. "Why would a good girl want you?"

But I insisted. What saved me were the *piyyutim* and *baqqashot*.

There was one girl they suggested me to, but she rejected the idea outright.

"Are you kidding?" she said. "He's not a *yeshivah bachur*."

"Come on Shabbat when he sings," they told her.

She came mostly because of the pressure put on her. After she heard me sing, she said, "He has a lofty soul. I'll turn him into a mensch."

She agreed to go out with me.

With my great character, I almost ruined everything.

Why? Because my private coin-operated phone was stolen.

Back then, there were no cell phones. People used pay phones, either public or private, where you dropped in a few coins and placed your call. I worked in a pizza parlor, and I bought one of these coin-operated phones to earn a little extra money. That very day, someone had stolen it from me.

I spent the whole date in a bad mood. She talked about building a home, and I talked about my stolen phone. She talked about a wedding, and I sat there with a Tishah B'Av face. I even tried to argue with the waiter, who brought a date-banana smoothie instead of banana-honey, but he was so courteous it was impossible to fight with him.

The girl told my friend who had made the suggestion, "He's tough."

At night, the friend called me and asked, "What's the answer?"

I was in the middle of counting the cash at the pizza place and answered, "I dunno."

"Just tell me, yes or no?"

"You know what? No!"

He gave her my answer.

I did everything to push away my happiness.

But Hashem is more powerful than anything.

The next Shabbat, she came again to hear the *piyyutim* and said, "Okay, I'll go out with him again."

We met, and then I realized that I'd been blind. I forgot all about the phone and pizza.

She told me I try to fool people by acting tough, but she heard the *piyyutim* and *baqqashot* and knew that such things can only come from someone with a lofty soul. I tried to tell her, "Nah, it's just something I've loved since I was a kid," to which she replied, "That's what I'm trying to tell you."

We got married. We've been married for sixteen years. She's an amazing wife. I finally got warmth and stability, kind words and admiration without any put downs—everything I never had before.

For years, I still didn't get along with my father.

On the Shabbat before the wedding, we almost came to blows.

Just minutes before the wedding, we argued. I didn't want to talk to him until one aunt made me do it.

Ten years into our marriage, my wife, with her womanly wisdom, brought about a reconciliation between my father and me. It took her a long time to convince me that my father wasn't a bad person, just a closed, very conventional man who didn't know how to get along with people.

Several months after I reconciled with him, he had a stroke and lost his ability to communicate with anyone. I was glad that Hashem had given me a chance to make up with him before it happened.

Since I've been working in a stable job all these years, as well as singing at weddings, I had the money to put out a disc of *piyyutim* four years ago. I am also a chazzan on the Yamim Tovim. *Baruch Hashem*, I'm earning a good living—nothing to brag about but enough to live on comfortably with a righteous woman, a woman of valor, and righteous children who give me a lot of *nachat*.

You like every story to have a message. I think there are a lot of messages in mine, but my biggest message is about the children. They say we tend to repeat things our parents did to us.

With *siyatta diShemaya*, with the help of my wife, I was able to do the opposite. I learned from my parents how not to act, how not to be too tough, how not to hold back from talking, how not to humiliate, exert pressure, and hurt.

I replaced humiliation with approval, silence with open

communication, toughness with deep love and warmth, and anxiety about their education with care and concern.

I don't deserve the credit. It all goes to the Creator of the World, Who gave me a wonderful wife. As well as a gift called *piyyutim* and *baqqashot*.

Wounded by a Friend

A strong friendship between two bachurim becomes even stronger. And from there, the road to dependency is short—yet at the same time, long and hard.

This is not just a story but a eye-opening look at the red flags for teens who may be confused by the difference between an ordinary friendship and emotional entanglement.

I haven't told my story to anyone since it happened ten years ago. I knew that when the time was right, I would share it, and I feel that time is now. Many fine people, especially teenagers, are dealing with what I dealt with. I'd like to let them learn from the lessons I paid such a high price for.

I come from a terrific family, with good, devoted parents. My childhood was wonderful. I can't point to any event or person that caused me harm or wronged me in any way. All in all, my life progressed in a manner I'd wish on everyone.

I was one of those naturally good children. I got good grades and never had any sort of trouble with the administration or with other children. You might be surprised to hear it, but there are children like that who never needed Chaim Walder or someone like him.

After graduating from eighth grade, I enrolled in a *yeshivah ketanah*, where I did well both socially and in learning. The three years I spent there were ones of growth and maturity, or so I thought.

Then I entered *yeshivah gedolah* at one of the best yeshivahs in the country.

I found my place both socially and in learning, and it looked that I would be repeating the success that always seemed to follow me.

At this yeshivah, I made a friend. We'll call him Binyamin (obviously, that's not his real name). He was talented. A special personality. Smart, pleasant, impeccable *middos*. I actually felt inferior to him right from the start because he really was perfect. Full of confidence. Charismatic. Fun to talk to. And on top of all that, he was a really good boy, a strong learner, and a *yarei Shamayim*. Like I said, perfect.

We became *chavrusos* and started to learn.

Our learning together was a powerful experience. We got a lot of pleasure out of learning together and it made us closer.

Yeshivah bachurim, like everyone else, have days where they struggle, where they find it hard to get up for davening, hard to learn, and they get into moods that are nothing to write home about.

A boy can find things hard for all sorts of reasons, and some can't pick themselves up. Others might take themselves in hand temporarily, yet the minute there's a crisis, they'll crash and burn.

Whenever I experienced a crisis, Binyamin helped me get through it. And when it happened to him, I was there for him in the same way.

If I got up late and started the day on the wrong foot, he'd come to me the next day with warm, kind words: "You know how special and wonderful you are, how much fun it is to learn with you, how much everyone admires you. You're a great boy with good *middos*, a real *lamdan*. I missed you."

Unwittingly, we bonded too strongly to each other. We felt that we were soaring in learning and *yiras shamayim*. We gave each other constant encouragement to grow stronger. We even joked that we didn't need the *mashgiach's mussar* talks because the strength we gave each other was stronger than anyone else could provide.

I have to say that it was true. A "talk" between him and me was worth ten talks from the *mashgiach*. Because I wanted to listen to him, and he wanted to listen to me.

I think this relationship gave both of us a sense of knowing that someone admired and appreciated him, and each thanked the other every moment.

My thanks were sincere. I really did admire him, and I thought he gave me a lot. Because that was the truth.

Unintentionally, we became dependent. Dependent on the spiritual high we felt we were getting from the other.

Of course, our friendship only got stronger. Everyone saw a winning pair that constantly strove and managed to rise and hold their heads above water in learning and behavior. It made a good impression, which certainly had implications socially. Our status was very high because in the yeshivah world, those who learn are valued.

But while I was happy and content, something was eating Binyamin up.

What I didn't know was that he had had a bad experience of dependency in *yeshivah ketanah*. While I innocently saw no problem with our relationship, he saw a major problem. He felt uncomfortable once he realized he couldn't do without me. I felt okay because I had no experience with dependency, so I was just enjoying our friendship.

I was naive, and I couldn't conceive of anything stronger than the bond the two of us had.

He spoke with one of the *rabbeim* in the yeshivah, who heard what he was feeling and said to him, "Tell him you must cut off all contact. Don't talk to him anymore."

Realizing that he was unable to do such a thing, he decided to share with me what he was going through.

He told me that he'd become dependent on me, and that it was as if he was enslaved to the relationship between us, and that if I were to tell him that I'd had enough of him, he'd go out of his mind and wouldn't be able to stand it.

I didn't know what he was talking about. I thought he was confused. "Why would I get tired of our friendship?" I asked in all innocence. "You're the best *chavrusa* I've ever had. You're my best friend, why should I get tired of it?"

It took him a few days to explain to me what was going on in his head, and so that I'd understand, he gave me a book written by a *bachur* (who's no longer alive). It's called *The Man in His World*, and it has a chapter called "The Destruction Caused by Dependency."

For the first time in my life, at age seventeen, I became acquainted with the concept of dependence.

At the yeshivah everyone was talking about our friendship because a yeshivah is a place where even the slightest movement is felt, but I innocently did not dream that all this was happening.

I felt like I was in a whirlpool. A black hole. In the midst of an explosion. I didn't know what to do with this information.

As a first step, he suggested that we stop being *chavrusas*.

That made waves in the yeshivah. I went along with it because he convinced me it was the right thing to do. The problem was, he obeyed the rosh yeshivah only partially. He cut off our spiritual connection but left open the channel of speech. And when you don't talk about learning and *yiras shamayim*, the only thing left to talk about is...

The connection.

Precisely during this period, when we began to talk about "how we need to separate," the dependent relationship became worse and turned problematic. We would sit together for hours talking about how we needed to separate and how hard it was. Unwittingly, an unhealthy bond was formed. Suddenly I saw things differently. I cared about who he was talking to and who he was becoming friends with, and he would calm me down and so on. And assure me we were still connected.

If there is one time in my life I would like to erase from memory, this is it.

Everything about him became magnified. Suddenly there was no longer learning, but obsession with what he thought of me and to what extent he was my friend—all kinds of thoughts that only made me feel worse.

From a calm boy, I became a tense, troubled boy. From a boy with a healthy personality, I found myself messed up, going from one extreme to the other, from being overjoyed to sinking into the pits of despair.

At this point, I did what Binyamin had done at the beginning of the end of the road.

I went to consult one of the yeshivah staff, who sent me to Rabbi Uri Brandwein, supervisor of the Chavat Daas Talmud Torah in Yerushalayim.

"There's not much to say," I told him. "Just tell me how to end the relationship."

Although he's a very busy man, he gave me plenty of time. He talked to me about dependency and how serious it is.

I asked him why something that made me feel so wonderful was bad, and he explained that the wonderful feeling did not come from me but was dependent on someone else and that depending on someone else diminishes my own strength.

He explained to me that we give children candy so they'll learn. The child is not interested in learning but in the prize. In the beginning, it's okay for him to associate the sweetness with learning. But if it continues, the child will actually relate more to the candy than to the learning.

"But the word *chaver*, friend, comes from the word *chibur*, connection, so what's the problem with that?" I asked him.

He replied that there really was no problem with connecting. "But you must realize that dependency changes you from a thinking person to a dependent person, from a powerful person to a powerless person. The power you feel is the power of others, not yours. You yourself don't have any power, and when he takes away your power, not only are you powerless, but you suffer as well because you feel completely empty."

I knew he was right. Because that's exactly how I felt.

At this stage, we cut off all contact. No messages were passed between us. It was really a process. This took place during the summer break. At first, the new situation didn't affect me at all. But in Elul, when I returned to yeshivah and saw him again, I began to feel how hard it was that he wasn't with me, and then I was sucked into a black hole that threatened my mental stability.

I'd be sitting next to him, but not talking to him. He was there, but not for me. Suddenly, all his smiles were for other people.

I was focused on what I didn't have and not on what I had. I began to hate him.

It was a Friday night, and I was in one of my rough moods. I decided to go to Yerushalayim and daven at the Kosel.

I arrived at the Kosel at eleven thirty, and said all of *sefer Tehillim* without once lifting my head from the *sefer*.

I don't remember ever having such a powerful experience.

With deep emotion, I said to Hashem, "I suddenly realize that my *emunah* is weak. I'm looking for friendship with a human being, forgetting that there is Someone close to me twenty-four hours a day, and that's You, Hashem. I am in Your hands. I trust You."

I recalled Abraham Fried's song, "Someone Is Always Walking with Me," and I said to Hashem: "Please, fill up this black hole of unhealthy friendship I'm in."

For the first time, I understood the words of our prayers, which emphasize feeling Hashem's closeness every minute of the day. Suddenly, I realized that all this time He was always there for me. All I had to do now was deepen my connection with Him and only Him.

I left at two in the morning with no idea how I was going to get back to the yeshivah. I didn't even know which way to leave. I left the Kosel plaza and walked out through Shaar Ashpot (Dung Gate), which left me in a dark, hostile place, trembling with fear.

Suddenly a commercial vehicle stopped. Inside was a religious driver.

"Hello, *bachur*," he called. "Are you sure you're not lost?"

"Can you take me to the entrance to the city?"

"No problem," he replied.

I got in the car. He didn't ask too many questions. He probably realized I was somewhat uneasy. We got to the entrance to the city, and he asked where I needed to go. I named the city where my yeshivah was located, and he said to me, "I'm going to the same place," and we continued to drive in silence.

When we arrived in the city he asked, "What yeshivah do you learn in?"

When I told him, he said, "You won't believe this, but I'm on my way there to deliver vegetables."

I found it hard to believe, but sure enough, when we arrived at 3:00 a.m., I watched as he unloaded the crates in the kitchen. I couldn't believe I'd gotten such a clear sign from Hashem, a sign of love and connection. It gave me tremendous encouragement and the realization that I'd done right thing in cutting off an unhealthy relationship to cling to Hashem.

That trip to the Kosel was the third stage. I was able to get out of the shock. I started the process of healing myself, which took me up to a whole new level.

Erev Rosh Hashanah, Binyamin sent me a message through another *bachur* asking my forgiveness. I said to the messenger, "Tell Binyamin I don't bear him any grudge because I know that everything he did was for my benefit. I know that, like it says in *Mishlei*, when a true friend gives me a blow, it stems from caring."

I also said to him, "Every night we daven in Maariv, '*Ahavas Olam*,' recognizing that Hashem's love for us is eternal. It's as if we're saying to Him, 'Though we might have caused You pain, You love us so much You can't be angry.' I can't be angry either. Thank him for me for sending regards. The main thing is that the separation was good for both of us."

That's my story. I'm sure thousands of *yeshivah bachurim* will be moved by it. Girls in seminary also struggle with destructive dependency that has some beautiful moments and lots of difficult moments, but which always ends badly. And if it doesn't end, that's even worse.

Today I am married and a father. Binyamin is also married and a father. We run into each other every so often and give each other a friendly hello. Yes, even today we both understand that we can never be friends.

Cast Your Wallet...

We've already discovered that if Rabbi Chaim Zayed leaves his house with a full wallet, chances are he'll lose it and discover a story in its place. But in this story, he loses his wallet twice in one day.

Which gives us two stories plus a surprising joint ending.

So here's another story about Rabbi Chaim Zayed, who's the closest thing to your Yerushalmi—only younger, more contemporary, and more Yemenite.

During the last vacation, Rabbi Zayed was invited to lecture to a group vacationing at the Carlton Hotel in Nahariya. He was asked to give two lectures a day over two days.

On the first day, Rabbi Zayed left his home and took the train to Nahariya.

He made do with a cup of coffee that morning, even skipping the cake. He did so for two reasons: one because he was in a rush to catch the train, and two, because he figured he'd be going to a hotel, not just an auditorium. Hotel breakfasts could last until noon or later. Before he began speaking, he'd go into the dining room and grab a bite to eat, as the organizers of the vacation package had offered meals as part of his payment.

He arrived at the hotel at exactly eleven, only to find the dining room empty. Why? Guess. So that everyone could attend the lecture of Rabbi Chaim Zayed.

"Hurry to the lecture room," his host said to him. "Everyone's been there waiting for you for almost a quarter of an hour."

"I guess that means there's no time for me to eat," Rabbi Zayed said.

"Absolutely not," the man replied. "People are waiting. But we'll get you a cup of coffee to tide you over until lunch."

Okay. Coffee was better than nothing. Rabbi Zayed entered and began his talk. It went over very well, and from time to time, he took a sip of coffee to give him the needed boost to continue.

The lecture ended with half of the audience surrounding Rabbi Zayed to ask his advice and receive a blessing, to say how much they enjoyed his lecture, and to ask questions. Why only half?

Because the other half had gone to eat lunch.

By the time the last person left, forty-five minutes had gone by. Rabbi Zayed remembered that he was hungry. He walked out of the lecture room toward the dining room only to find that lunch had ended ten minutes earlier, and the dining room was locked.

As if that wasn't enough, the organizer urged him forward. "The second lecture is going to start late because you answered all those questions. We're behind schedule."

"Is there anything to drink?" Rabbi Zayed asked.

"Sure. I'll see that they bring you a black coffee."

Rabbi Zayed had seen black for quite a while. He entered the lecture hall and began to speak. Never had a lecture been given with such a huge contrast between the lecturer's mood and body and the audience's mood and bodies.

While his audience was full and attentive, enjoying every moment and laughing at all the right places, Rabbi Zayed was hungry and dizzy, wondering whether to faint or smile. In the end, he chose the latter option.

The second lecture ended at six-thirty and was greeted by another round of applause followed by a deluge of well-wishers, advice seekers, and fans until a glance at his watch told him it was time to leave. Otherwise, he'd miss his train home.

He left and then remembered that he hadn't eaten a thing that day. Dinner would be at eight, but he couldn't wait for it. He asked if there was a kosher takeout place nearby, and it turned out that there was one in Nahariya with the best kashrus certification.

He had half an hour until the train was scheduled to leave, so he decided to go buy a meal, even though he doesn't usually enter restaurants and takeout places.

He entered the place and saw a sign that said, "Business lunch for 39.90." He walked up to the counter and placed his order.

He reached into his pocket for his wallet, and—

Let's pause for a moment to remember that this is a story about Rabbi Zayed. No one expects the wallet to be there, correct? Otherwise, where's the story?

So, he didn't take out his wallet. Why? Because it wasn't there.

Where could my wallet be? he wondered. *Was it stolen? Maybe on the train? In the taxi? At the hotel?* Suddenly he remembered that no one had stolen his wallet. It was back home right where he'd left it, on his dresser.

"That'll be thirty-nine ninety, Rabbi," the man behind the counter said.

What am I going to say to him? That I have no money? Then why am I standing here?

He decided to conduct a search.

Because Rabbi Zayed is a rabbi, besides his pants and shirt, he also wears a frock coat and carries a briefcase. He started to search for any stray cash that might have been tucked away somewhere in a place that wasn't a wallet. He discovered pockets he didn't know he had and others whose existence he wasn't sure of.

In the tenth pocket or so, he came across a couple of pieces of paper. Guess what? On each was written twenty shekels.

He had the exact amount he needed to pay for a satisfying meal, without even half a shekel left over for a drink.

His hunger made everything look and sound different. Just the smell of the food made him feel faint.

He awaited his turn stoically. The person in front of him was being served, and soon his awful hunger would be a thing of the past.

Right then, a strange-looking person entered the place. He looked around, and his gaze settled on Rabbi Zayed.

"I see that you are a rabbi," he said. "I want you to do me a favor."

"How can I help you, my son?" Rabbi Zayed said to him.

"I have to go to Tel Aviv, but I got stuck without money. I need the rabbi to give me money for the trip."

"How much does the trip cost?" Rabbi Zayed asked him, figuring he could order a cheaper meal.

"Thirty-nine shekels," the man replied.

Rabbi Zayed felt like he was going to faint, and not for the first time that day.

According to halachah, he knew that he didn't have to give his money to the man. He'd reached a place of *pikuach nefesh*. As he was weighing his options, the man said to him, "Rabbi, please. It's a mitzvah. How can you say no to a Jew in need?"

There are usually ways to check if the Jew is in need or not, and if he even wants to travel to Tel Aviv or just take you for a ride.

The simple method: You take a hundred-shekel bill out of your wallet and say to the man who only asks for "a loan or a gift" because he got stuck, "Do you have change for a hundred?"

If he's a con artist, he'll look at your hundred-shekel bill and reply without thinking, "No problem, no problem. I've got change."

To which you reply, "Great, then you can use the change to travel."

But this time Rabbi Zayed did not have a hundred shekels or even a wallet. He also wasn't familiar with this trick against con artists, and because he is Rabbi Zayed, an expert in miracles and stories that don't always conform to reason, he realized that this was the beginning of a story whose end was unclear and that there must be a reason why the Creator of the World had starved him for half a day and was now giving him a bonus test by tempting him with delicious food that emitted a tantalizing aroma. Something was going on, and he wasn't about to miss his chance.

But in order not to miss it, he'd have to miss his meal, the likes of which he hadn't eaten since the day before.

Yet that's exactly what he did.

To make sure that the money was being used for its purported purpose, he pulled out the two twenties and said to the man, "Come with me. I'll pay your fare."

The man readily joined him. They reached the train station. Rabbi Zayed used his round-trip ticket for himself and paid the fare of the strange Jew, receiving half a shekel's change.

On the way, they talked. The Jew asked his name, and the rabbi replied, "My name is Chaim Zayed."

"Tell me something," the man asked. "Aren't you hungry?"

"Not anymore," he replied. By now, he felt on the level of an angel, for only angels can get along without food.

The train arrived at the Savidor station in Tel Aviv, and each went his own way.

Rabbi Zayed arrived home and finally had a satisfying meal.

"You eat like you're after a fast," his wife said. "Is everything okay?

"I didn't fast," the rabbi replied. "I drank three cups of coffee." At the look she gave him, he asked for a fourth cup and told her the events of the day. Any woman would be shaken up at hearing such things, but she's Rabbi Zayed's wife, isn't she? By now, no story, no matter how strange, will rattle her.

If you thought the day was over, well, that's just it. Like the story, both were just getting started.

After dinner, the Rabbi's son came over to him and said, "Abba, do you remember that you promised me we'd go to the pool together during vacation?"

Rabbi Zayed tried to get out of it. "How about going with your friends?"

"Abba, I have plenty of friends but only one father. Please come with me."

Rabbi Zayed shrugged his shoulders or what was left of them after his grueling day.

They drove to the pool, and when they got to the changing room, he realized that he'd made the opposite mistake of what he'd done that morning. In the morning, he'd left his wallet at home, and now he'd forgotten to leave it at home. It was right there in his pocket.

Every pool regular knows that you never bring your wallet to the pool, even if it only has twenty shekels in it. In Rabbi Zayed's wallet, unlike the usual amount, there were two thousand eight hundred shekels in cash plus credit cards as well as a promissory note for a large sum, money owed to him by someone who'd been avoiding paying him and was most likely praying that the note would disappear, and with it, proof of the debt. Apparently, Rabbi Zayed thought, the debtor's prayer was about to be answered.

Rabbi Zayed looked around for a locker in which to store personal items, but instead of lockers, he saw huge warning notices posted: "The pool is not responsible for the loss or theft of personal items." Other notices warned against thieves in the area. Rabbi Zayed realized that leaving his wallet in his pocket, or anywhere else, and going into the pool, would be like giving a free gift to those lowly people who'd pounce on his wallet, as well as saying a final goodbye to the debt that he had already been close to saying Kaddish over.

"You know what?" he said to his son. "I don't think I'll be going in the pool. I'll watch you, and we'll be together, okay?"

The son gave his father a look reserved solely for fathers who are about to do this to their children again. "You can't do this to me," the boy said. "You run all over the world helping people. I also want a father who swims with me and splashes water on me."

Rabbi Zayed recognized defeat when he saw it. No way could he not get in the pool.

With a heavy heart, he began to think about all kinds of hiding places. Then an original thought came to his mind, or at least that's what he thought at that moment: *I'll take off my shoes, push my wallet into a shoe as deeply as possible, and then...* He almost smiled at the brilliance of it. *And then, I'll stuff my socks in it, the ones I've been wearing all day. Even if it occurs to anyone to think of this hiding place, the location would certainly put him off.*

And so, Rabbi Zayed joined his son, and they both jumped into the pool and swam and enjoyed it immensely. The swim made Rabbi Zayed forget all the trials and tribulations of the day, the hunger, the strange fellow who needed a train ticket, and, of course, the wallet.

Two hours later, they returned to the changing room. As they entered, Rabbi Zayed remembered his wallet. He ran to the shoes, stuck his hand inside one, and came across a sock. *Good*, he thought happily. But his joy lasted exactly half a minute because under the sock was supposed to be a wallet. But the wallet had obviously decided to swim away. In fact, someone had decided to fish it out, and that someone was kind enough to put the sock back in its place.

Two thousand eight hundred shekels, credit cards, and a debt that had just been wiped off the books.

What a tough day.

Rabbi Zayed ran to the lifeguard and the pool manager, asking them to replay the camera footage.

"There are no cameras," they told him. "There are signs here instead of cameras."

Rabbi Zayed didn't say anything about this to his son so as not to ruin the mood more than it was already ruined.

He arrived home despondent and told his wife what had happened. Though she is Rabbi Zayed's wife and already accustomed to stories, a strange story is one thing, but losing a wallet with a lot of money and credit cards and a debt that was long overdue was another.

They sat, trying to come up with a plan.

"We have to place our faith in Hashem," Rabbi Zayed told his wife. "This loss was decreed for us from Above, and there's nothing to do."

At midnight, Rabbi Zayed retired for the night, exhausted.

At 1:00 a.m. his cellphone rang.

"Good evening, Rabbi Zayed, are you awake?"

"I am now," Rabbi Zayed gave his standard reply to those who called in the middle of the night and after managing to rouse him asked if he was awake. A sort of grim confirmation. "Who's speaking?"

"Come on, don't you remember me?"

Now the anonymous caller wanted Rabbi Zayed to remember him. He wasn't sure if he should.

"It's me, Yochai, from the Nahariya train, the one whose ticket you paid for."

If there were a list of people that Rabbi Zayed didn't want to hear about anymore, this man would be the first on the list.

"How can I help you?"

"Tell me something. Did you lose your wallet?"

"What?!" Rabbi Zayed shouted and wanted to add, "Did you steal my wallet?" Fortunately, by now, his mind was alert, something that couldn't be said about the rest of him, and he recalled that his wallet was not in a position to be stolen when they'd met.

"How did you get my wallet?"

"I'll tell you. Right now I'm on a bus to Holon. I was sitting up front in the first seat next to the driver. A guy with a ponytail got on, put his Rav Kav on the machine to pay, and kept on walking.

"'Do me a favor, pal,' the driver said to me. 'The guy forgot his Rav Kav. Bring it to him, okay?'"

"I looked at the Rav Kav and saw it had a picture of you. I said to myself, 'Hold it. What's with that rabbi? This morning, he had a beard, and now he has a ponytail? What's going on here?' I couldn't figure it out.

"But after thinking about it again, I got suspicious. And then I thought—something I don't do too much of—and then it dawned on me that this guy is not Rabbi Zayed at all.

"Once I came to that conclusion, I said to myself, 'Wait a minute. Did Rabbi Zayed give this guy his Rav Kav? It can't be, because the religious think that's stealing.' Then I considered that maybe the guy borrowed the Rav Kav from you without asking you about it ahead of time. You following?"

"I'm trying to," Rabbi Zayed said.

"So I went over to the guy casually, not giving anything away, and said to him, 'Are you Rabbi Zayed?' He didn't want to answer. He didn't say yes, and he didn't say no. He didn't want me to know the answer. But I already knew the answer from this morning, so I said to him, '*Chabibi*, either you tell me where you got this Rav Kav, or I'm calling the police.'

"Don't get me wrong, Rabbi. I just said that, but I'd never call the police. It doesn't go like that in our neighborhood. But I said it to him to make him talk, you understand, Rabbi? Maybe some information would slip out. So he answered me, 'Drop it. I found a wallet, and the card was in it.'

"'You found a wallet, huh?' I said to him. 'Wait right here. I know Rabbi Zayed. The man paid my train fare from Nahariya today instead of buying himself food.'

"At this point, I realized he was going to run away, so I told him, 'Listen to me, and listen good. If you make one move to leave, then the police will be the *best* thing that happens to you today.' He made a quick calculation about what I'd said and decided he shouldn't even look like someone who was about to move. Now I'm calling you, Rabbi. Tell me what I should do with this guy? I'll do whatever you say."

"First of all," Rabbi Zayed told him, "check the wallet to see how much money is in it."

The guy checked and reported back. "There are credit cards and papers."

"Any bills?"

"No, no bills."

"There were two thousand eight hundred shekels in the wallet."

"Empty out your pockets, because I'm not that good at emptying," Rabbi Zayed heard Yochai say diplomatically.

"Hold on, Rabbi. He's emptying them. There's a sea of blues [two-hundred shekel notes], Rabbi. Let me count."

He counted.

"I see here thirteen blues and one yellow of a hundred. One hundred shekels is missing."

The thief took twenty-five shekels out of his pocket and said, "I bought candy and a few other things."

"What to do, Rabbi?"

"Let it go," Rabbi Zayed said. "The fact that he touched my socks is his greatest punishment. He deserves a hundred shekels compensation. Just see if the credit cards are there and if there's a promissory note inside."

Yochai checked. "Yes, Rabbi, there are three credit cards and a handwritten IOU, plus the blues and the yellow. What now?"

"Warn the fellow. Just to make sure, take his name and address. If you can, take a taxi and come to my house. I'll repay you."

Within half an hour, Yochai was at Rabbi Zayed's house in Bnei Brak.

They sat at the kitchen table and argued a bit, the Rabbi and Yochai, because the Rabbi wanted to give him five hundred shekels as a reward and Yochai refused. In the end, he agreed to accept two hundred and a taxi back.

"I'll tell you the truth. I won't lie," Yochai told the Rabbi. "Usually, I wouldn't get involved. If a guy found a wallet, let him find it. It's none of my business. But what you did for me made it personal. You weren't just some anonymous person.

You helped me, even at the expense of your own food. I acted here as if it was my own wallet."

They parted in friendship, in the dead of night, and if, during the day, Rabbi Zayed had wondered why the Creator arranged the day the way He had, now everything was clear. Every test sent us by Hashem has meaning, purpose, and reward.

Glossary

The following glossary provides a partial explanation of some of the Hebrew, Yiddish (Y.), and words in other languages used in this book. The spellings and explanations reflect the way the specific word is used herein. Often, there are alternate spellings and meanings for the words.

achi: lit., "my brother"; said to a fellow Jew to express closeness.
adoni: sir
a"h: acronym for *aleha hashalom* (peace unto her), added to the name of the deceased.
aktion: Nazi operation of rounding up and killing Jews
aravos: willow branches; one of the four species waved together on Succos.
avreich (pl. *avreichim*): young married Torah student

b'ezras Hashem: G-d willing
baal tefillah: chazzan
baalas teshuvah: a formerly nonobservant Jewish woman or girl who has returned to Jewish tradition and practice
bachur (pl. *bachurim*): a young man; a yeshivah student.

baqqashot: lit., "requests." A collection of traditional supplications, songs, and prayers sung by Sephardic communities on Shabbat

baruch Hashem: "Thank G-d!"

b'chasdei Shamayim: with Hashem's mercy

bein adam l'chaveiro: interpersonal relations

bein hazemanim: the yeshivah intercession

beis din (pl. *battei din*): a rabbinical court(s) of law

beis medrash: study hall

ben Torah: lit., "son of Torah"; one who learns Torah.

b'ezras Hashem: with G-d's help

bimah: the reader's desk in in the synagogue on which the Torah scroll is opened and read

birkas kohanim: The kohen's blessings recited in the morning prayers during the chazzan's repetition of the Shemoneh Esrei

chag (pl. *chagim*): a holiday

chalakah: The traditional haircutting a Jewish boy receives when he turns three, which leaves him with the required side curls prescribed by the Torah

chareidi (pl. chareidim): an ultra-Orthodox Jew

chesed: acts of kindness

chabibi: slang for "buddy"

chavrusas: study partners

chiloni: a Jew who does not keep mitzvos

chol hamoed: the intermediate days of a festival

davka: (Y.) specifically that

dvar Torah (pl. *divrei Torah*): words of Torah

ein od Milvado: "there is none but Him (G-d)"

Eishes Chayil: "Woman of Valor"; song traditionally sung at the Shabbos evening meal.

emunah: faith in G-d.

erev Shabbos: the hours on Friday evening before the onset of Shabbos

gemach: acronym for "*gemilas chassadim*"; a place where items are lent free of charge.
gestorben (Y.): died
Geveret: Lady

hakafos: dancing with the Torah on Simchas Torah
Hashem: G-d
hashgachah, *hashgachah pratis*: Divine Providence
hekdesh: assests designated for a sacred purpose only and therefore cannot be sold or give away for another purpose
Hodu laShem ki tov: Give thanks to G-d for He is good

Kabbalas Shabbos: the prayers said on Friday night to welcome Shabbos
kabbalos: vows that one accepts upon himself
kahal: congregation.
kallah: lit., "bride"; daughter-in-law.
kapparah: an atonement
kiddush Hashem: sanctification of God's Name
Kim ahere! (Y.): "Come here!"
kimcha d'Pischa: lit, charity given before Pesach to help provide for the holiday's needs.
kippah: a skullcap, yarmulke.
kiruv: returning nonreligious Jews to their heritage
koishiklach (Y): holders woven from palm tree leaves, and used for the four species waved on Succos.
Kol mevaser, mevaser v'omer: the prayer receited at the end of Hoshana Rabbah while beating the myrtle branches on the ground, a custom instituted by the Prophets.
kollel: a center for advanced Torah study for adult students, mostly married men.
Kosel: the Western Wall

lamdan: an accomplisted Torah student
leibedik (Y.): lively

lashon hara: speaking badly about another Jew
leining: reading the weekly Torah portion during communal prayers

mashgiach: a spiritual guide in a yeshivah
middos: character traits
mikvah: a pool for ritual immersion
motza'ei Shabbos: after Shabbos

nachas, nachat: pride, satisfaction, pleasure.
neshamah: (lit.) "soul"
nusach: variation of the text of prayer

oiy vavoy (Y.): "How terrible!"

paroches: the curtain that covers the ark, which contains the Torah scrolls.
paytanim: those who sing *piyyutim*
pikuah nefesh: a matter of life or death
piyyutim: liturgical songs
potches (Y.): light slaps
psak din: a rabbinic court's final verdict

rasha: an evil person
r"m: abbreviation for "*rosh mesivta*"
rosh mesivta: head of a yeshivah
ruach hakodesh: Divine inspiration

savlanut: patience
savta: grandmother
seder: learning session in a yeshivah consisting of several hours
sefarim: sacred books
sefer Tehillim: the Book of Psalms
segulah: a supralogical action that has practical effects.
seudah, seudos: a meal(s)